Prague

A guide to twentieth-century architecture

...

Ivan Margolius
Photographs by Keith Collie

Prague

A guide to twentieth-century architecture

● ● ● ellipsis KÖNEMANN

• • •

Prague: a guide to twentieth-century architecture

CREATED, EDITED AND DESIGNED BY
Ellipsis London Limited
55 Charlotte Road London EC2A 3QT
E MAIL ...@ellipsis.co.uk
WWW http://www.ellipsis.co.uk/ellipsis
PUBLISHED IN THE UK AND AFRICA BY
Ellipsis London Limited
SERIES EDITOR Tom Neville
SERIES DESIGN Jonathan Moberly
LAYOUT Pauline Harrison

COPYRIGHT © 1996 Könemann
Verlagsgesellschaft mbH
Bonner Str. 126, D-50968 Köln
PRODUCTION MANAGER Detlev Schaper
PRINTING AND BINDING Sing Cheong
Printing Ltd
Printed in Hong Kong

ISBN 3 89508 282 1 (Könemann)
ISBN 1 899858 18 0 (Ellipsis)

Ivan Margolius 1996

Contents

Hradčany to Nové Město 17
Vinohrady to Vyšehrad 127
Žižkov and Vinohrady 157
Podolí to Hodkovičky 169
Smíchov to Hlubočepy 183
Hradčany to Ruzyně 201
Holešovice to Troja 239
Ďáblice to Hostivař 271
Biographies 293
Index 305

Introduction

When describing the city of Prague it is difficult to avoid superlatives. It is certainly an overwhelming capital on the one hand, demanding constant attention so that nothing is missed, and on the other, totally relaxing as Prague's urban structure, its buildings, streets, squares, parks and its broad valley setting on the river have a human scale which is comforting, intimate and embracing. Primarily the high quality of architecture contributes to the overall effect.

Buildings of diverse architectural styles and periods are arranged like theatrical scenery. Smaller buildings are placed in front of large, broad and plain ones are jammed against thin and exuberant ones, modern, hard-edged structures mingle with soft Baroque or Secessionist façades, layering themselves into a mixed but comprehensible harmony of space and form. The silhouettes of towers and church spires are outlined against a backdrop of wavy, red clay-tiled roofs. In winter, smoke from stoves burning brown coal (green environmental policies are only slowly being implemented) mixes with patches of mist permeating the narrow streets. At night Prague gains yet another dimension when the floodlights sharpen architectural details against the dark shadows.

Our aim is to explore the 20th century architecture of Prague, of which there are over 1500 noteworthy buildings, including works by Adolf Loos, Jože Plečnik, Bruno Paul and Mart Stam. As in any other city, Prague's historical development is important in the understanding of its complexity, character and the reasons for its growth over the years, and therefore it is necessary to describe the main stages of its evolution.

Prague, a natural centre of the European continent, grew at the cross-roads of the ancient trading routes. Prague Castle was founded between 880 and 890 as the permanent seat of the Czech Přemysl princes on a hill above the Vltava river. Church and monastery buildings were built within the Castle walls and a town started to develop below, on the banks of the river. Main activities were concentrated on the central town market held on the present Staroměstské náměstí (Old Town Square). The Staré Město (Old Town) was fortified at the beginning of the 13th century and Malá Strana (Lesser Quarter) was officially founded in 1257 on the left bank below the Castle.

The Roman Emperor Charles IV made Prague his home between 1346 and 1378 and had enormous influence on the development of the city. He founded Prague University in 1348 and established Nové Město (New Town) in the same year. Construction of the Charles Bridge, across the Vltava, was started in 1357 and building of the city landmark, the Gothic St Vitus Cathedral, began in 1344, replacing the previous Romanesque basilica.

At the beginning of the 15th century Jan Hus, a Czech religious reformer influenced by the writings of the Englishman John Wycliffe, preached in Betlémská Chapel against ecclesiastical abuses and encouraged the use of Czech rather than Latin in church sermons. His views tempted armed conflicts between German and Czech supporters of the Pope and the Protestant Hussite followers.

In 1526 the Czech crown passed to the Austrian house of Hapsburg. Uprisings which followed lost Prague citizens their political independence and resulted in the suppression of Czech language and culture. In 1618, the famous defenestration of Prague took place when the enraged Protestant nobles threw two Catholic councillors from the windows of Prague Castle into the moat. Nobody was seriously hurt but the incident marked the outbreak of the Thirty Years' War. After the battle at Bílá hora (White Mountain) near Prague in 1620, at which the Protestant Czech nobility lost to the Austrian Catholic forces of Ferdinand II, the situation deteriorated further and many Czechs left the country, including important personalities and artists like Jan Amos Comenius and Wenceslas Hollar. The Emperor's court and the administrative offices moved to Vienna and Prague stagnated into a second-rate city. Nevertheless, Praguers endeavoured, together with a number of foreign artists and architects who settled there under Hapsburg patronage, to keep developing and expanding the city especially after a large fire in 1689. It was at this time that Baroque churches and palaces were built, including the city fortifications. In 1784 four independent towns, Staré Město, Nové Město, Malá Strana and Hradčany were officially incorporated, forming one urban entity.

At local elections in 1861 the Czech political parties won over the Austrian opposition and again established themselves as the dominant force in their city. This change enabled Czech artists and professionals to build in Prague and to elevate it from its provincial status to a large European metropolis. They started by planning and erecting buildings to revive the Czech culture and spirit: the National Theatre, the National Museum, the House of Artists (Rudolfinum) and the Czech Institute of Technology. Rules regulating the town planning of the city were established and the Building Act of 1886 set the maximum height of buildings to 'six quarters' of the street width with a limit of five storeys. The major urban planning issues were decided by the Artistic Commission, instituted in 1896, together with the Prague city council. The most important aspects were determined by competitions, for example, the slum clearance of Staré Město, the transportation connection for Letná Plain and Staré Město and the urban renewal of Nové Město.

The influence of new directions in art and architecture starting with the Art Nouveau/Secession style, came to Bohemia at the beginning of this century through artists' trips abroad, their studies and exhibitions held in the city. In the summer of 1902, Mánes, an important group of artists, organised a show of Auguste Rodin's sculptures and, in 1905, an exhibition of Edvard Munch's paintings took place. These two events had an enormous influence on the future development of Czech modern art.

Czech architects were inspired by cultural influences from abroad but also sought to develop their own distinct direction. Following the Secession Movement, Modernist tendencies evolved influenced by the works of Hendrik Petrus Berlage and Frank Lloyd Wright. Then, with the sudden emergence of Cubist paintings in France, Czechs applied this trend to architecture, and created unique Cubist buildings, concentrated mostly in Prague. After the First World War, in 1918, the Austro-Hungarian Empire broke up and the Czechoslovak Republic was founded. The Cubist influence, mixed with nationalistic folklore, continued for a short time until the new inspiration arrived from France and Germany to dominate creativity in the 1920s and 1930s. In 1920 the avant-garde Devětsil movement was established, greatly affecting the artistic community. Devětsil became a platform for functional Modernism, forming a programme for a new approach to architecture, design, photography, film, literature and music.

Many of the innovative buildings erected in Prague were illustrated in international publications, initiating visits by foreign artists. Writers and architects like André Breton, Adolf Loos, Mart Stam, Henry van de Velde, F.R.S. Yorke, Frank Yerbury, and Le Corbusier recognised early in their careers that Prague was an ideal meeting place for admirers and students of modern art and architecture and encouraged others to visit. Berlage, Raymond Unwin, J.J.P. Oud, Walter Gropius, Amédée Ozenfant, Theo van Doesburg, André Lurçat and Hannes Meyer gave lectures; some also visited other Czech cities and even left built projects. Mies van der Rohe's

Prague: a guide to twentieth-century architecture

Villa Tugendhat is in Brno, Erich Mendelsohn's Bachner Department Store was built in Ostrava, Adolf Loos's Villa Müller and Villa Winternitz and Mart Stam's Villa Palička are in Prague. Jože Plečnik was involved in the renovation of Prague Castle and built the Sacred Heart Church in Prague. Peter Behrens, J.J.P. Oud, Le Corbusier, Marcel Breuer and Johannes Duiker participated in various competitions and unrealised projects.

The Munich pact sealed the fate of Czechoslovakia. Bohemia and Moravia were occupied by Germany for the duration of the Second World War and Slovakia became an independent fascist state. After the war, in 1948, the Communist Party took over the country. Under the oppressive regime that followed links with the Western world were severed and the progress of technology and culture faltered. Architectural creativity also suffered not only due to the forced realignment with the Soviet-led Socialist Realism but also due to lack of private investment and the rigid, centrally governed economy. Typical products of that period are the Hotel International (František Jeřábek, 1952–56) at Koulova Street and Hotel Jalta (Antonín Tenzer, 1954–55) on Wenceslas Square. Dubček's 'Socialism with a Human Face' lasted only eight months and had little effect on the development of architecture. The Soviet occupation on 21 August 1968 caused the loss of intellectuals, who fled the country, and the political grip tightened.

Centralised policies enforced the continued sprawl of grey, uniform housing estates (sídliště) built in concrete panel systems which quickly closed around the capital. Major planning decisions were made without due regard to the fabric of the city. The north–south, six-lane dual carriageway, magistrála (1975–78), which cuts into the heart of the city abruptly ending at top of Wenceslas Square, is a prime example of that folly. Other projects resulted in faceless, unsuitable and domineering buildings with no reference or response to their location within Prague's urban texture. To this category belong the Orwellian Parliament building next to the National Museum (Karel Prager, 1966–72), the colossal Palace of Culture at Vyšehrad (Jaroslav Mayer, Vladimír Ustohal, Antonín Vaněk, Josef Karlík, 1976–80), the alien skyscraper office and hotel blocks mainly concentrated in Nusle and Michle, the Thunderbirds-rocket-like Žižkov radio jamming and TV tower (Václav Aulický, 1985–1988) and the characterless Hotel HiltonAtrium at Pobřežní Street (Stanislav Franc, Jan Nováček, Vladimír Fencl, 1988–90). However, occasionally more fitting schemes and projects were realised, for instance the Villa Chytilová in Troja, the Tennis Stadium at Štvanice and the Speech Therapy Clinic in Smíchov.

Since November 1989, with the fall of Communism, a new era of openness has begun for the country and its capital. Financial investment and business opportunities have helped to establish a healthy atmosphere for growth, creating an explosion of construction activity in Prague. Old buildings are being adapted and converted. New buildings are being erected within the tight inner courtyards and on a few sites left empty since the war. The speed of building is fast and furious and sometimes detrimental to the quality of architecture. The scene has opened for well-known foreign architects to build in Prague, Frank Gehry and Claude Parent being the first.

During the early 1990s Czech architects caught up on missed chances, being seduced firstly by Post-modernism, typical examples being the tacky Hotel Hoffmeister (Petr Keil, 1990–93) at Chotkova Street and the grotesque Hotel Don Giovanni (Ivo Nahálka, 1993–94) at Vinohradská. However, it will not be long before Czech architects begin to develop their

Prague: a guide to twentieth-century architecture

own distinct styles to match the quality of the buildings their predecessors built during the inter-war period.

The historical centre of Prague is a Class 1 conservation area and is included in UNESCO's list of World Cultural Monuments. Some buildings are currently in poor condition but, under the new restitution laws, and if money is available, they will be renovated and redecorated. This process will take some time. Do not be disappointed if some of the buildings are looking a little sad.

Even though most of the buildings listed in this guide are protected by the Czech heritage laws these are rather ineffectual. Now new owners who acquire buildings threaten to destroy the original interiors and exteriors. These have survived unaltered the ravages of the World Wars and the Communist regime (which, in fact, prevented all the capitalist business dealings normally encountered in free societies and therefore unintentionally helped to preserve Prague's architectural heritage) only to fall to the ruthless pressures and fast profits of the new breed of Czech entrepreneurs.

Despite the limited selection of around 120 examples, the range of buildings illustrated in this guide will suffice to show the richness and variety of modern architecture to be found in Prague.

ACKNOWLEDGEMENTS

For helping to make this book possible thanks go to: Amanda Bates for
3D modelling, comments, support and proof-reading, Keith Collie for
photography and companionship, Jan Kaplický for sources of information and advice, Zdeněk Lukeš for arranging access to buildings and for
comments, Heda Margolius Kovaly for translations and corrections, Jiří
Horský for the latest updates, the National Technical Museum, the Czech
Museum of Fine Arts and the Museum of National Literature for letting
us photograph their buildings and reproduce images from their archives,
Jonathan Moberly and Tom Neville for having the idea of publishing this
series of guides, and a number of owners who allowed us to photograph
their buildings and entertained us over coffee and cakes, revealing more
of their houses' history.

IM November 1995

Prague: a guide to twentieth-century architecture

Using this book

The guide is divided into eight sections. Each section is based on a Prague borough, the last section combining three districts. Currently Greater Prague consists of ten boroughs of differing sizes. The buildings are arranged along a route around each borough.

Prague is a relatively small city and is easily covered on foot, especially within the historical centre. Public transport systems – metro, trams and buses – are clean, efficient and incredibly cheap. Tickets have to be bought before travelling from tobacconists or metro stations. Avoid using taxis which can be very expensive for tourists. A good city map of 1:20,000 scale is recommended and is obtainable from bookshops or newspaper kiosks. At most times you will find an English-speaking person to help you reach your intended destination should you get lost on the way.

In Prague each building carries two numbers. The blue number is a sequential number in the street. The red number (*číslo popisné*) is the sequential number of the building in the district in which it is situated. In this guide the blue number is given first. The street (*ulice*), avenue (*třída*), square (*náměstí*), market (*trh*), or embankment (*nábřeží*) names are displayed on attractive enamel plaques at each end or corner.

In order to make a choice of buildings for this book a great number of buildings had to be set aside. Where there is another interesting building near the listed one, it is mentioned at the end of the description. Building titles contain the names of the original clients and their original intended use. For ease of using local maps all addresses are given in Czech.

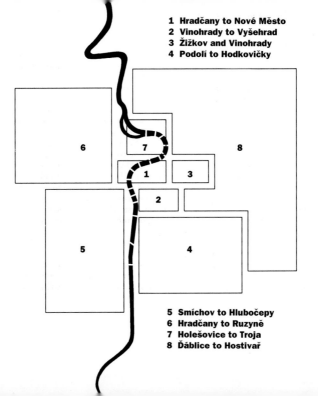

1 Hradčany to Nové Město
2 Vinohrady to Vyšehrad
3 Žižkov and Vinohrady
4 Podolí to Hodkovičky

5 Smíchov to Hlubočepy
6 Hradčany to Ruzyně
7 Holešovice to Troja
8 Ďáblice to Hostivař

Reconstruction of Prague Castle 18
Completion of St Vitus Cathedral 24
Tombs of Czech Kings 26
Reconstruction of the Theresian Wing, Prague Castle 28
Orangery 30
Malostranská Metro Station 32
Svatopluk Čech Bridge (most Svatopluka Čecha) 34
Memorial to the Victims of Communism 36
Cooperative Housing 38
Office Building, Liliová 40
Štenc House 42
Extension to Charles University 44
'At the Black Madonna' Department Store 46
Municipal House (Obecní dům) 48
'At the God's Eye' House 50
Merkur Palace 52
Bílá Labuť Department Store 54
Bank of the Czechoslovak Legions 56
Assicurazioni Generali & Moldavia Generali Building 58
Myslbek Development 60
Bondy Department Store and Černá Růže Arcade 62
Department Store, Provaznická 64
ČKD Building 66
ARA Department Store 68
Retail and Apartment Building, Jungmannovo náměstí 70
Music Store 72

Hradčany to Nové Město

Riunione Adriatica di Sicurta Palace 74
Škoda Works Administrative Building 76
Urbánek House 78
Koruna Palace 80
Lindt Department Store 82
Lamp Post 84
Baťa Department Store 86
Peterka Department Store 88
Hotel Juliš 90
U Stýblů Building and Alfa Arcade 92
Grand Hotel Evropa and Hotel Meran 94
Moravian Bank 96
Edison Transformer 98
Brno Bank 100
Habich Building 102
Apartment Buildings and Arcade 104
Lucerna Palace 106
U Nováků Palace 108
Retail and Apartment Building, Palackého 110
Diamant House and Arch 112
Olympic Building 114
Czechoslovak Decorative Arts Federation Building 116
Máj Department Store, now K-Mart 118
Nová Scéna National Theatre 120
Hlahol House 122
Mánes Building 124

Reconstruction of Prague Castle

At the end of the last century, Slovenian architect Jože Plečnik studied with a Czech, Jan Kotěra, at Otto Wagner's studio at the Academy of Fine Arts in Vienna. They became friends, their Slavonic background bringing them together. In 1911 Kotěra invited Plečnik to Prague to take up a professorship at the Institute of Decorative Arts. Ten years later Plečnik left for a similar post in Ljubljana, but not before Czechoslovak President Tomáš Garrigue Masaryk rewarded him for his long teaching period in Prague by commissioning him to renovate and reconstruct Prague Castle.

Plečnik was an exceptional architect, influenced by the writings of Gottfried Semper and inspired by the classical architecture of antiquity from which he adopted elements and forms establishing his own distinctive style, reflecting his feelings for human existence and his religious convictions. Plečnik used architecture to convey his symbolic and spiritual messages and one cannot pass any of his work without pausing for admiration.

The best way to see Plečnik's work is to start at the First Courtyard[1] off the Hradčanské náměstí. The tall 25-metre flagpoles are Plečnik's contribution.

Before entering the Second Courtyard look left through the well-detailed, glazed, bronze gates into the stunning Plečnik Hall. You will see Plečnik's 'signature' of a column placed in front of a circular opening.[2]

Through a passage to the left in the Second Courtyard is the Bastion Garden[3] designed by Plečnik. Note the circular steps with the fountain and the stone balustrade along the walkway to the Powder Bridge.

Walk through the Second Courtyard and on to the Third Courtyard, where you will find 'architect-designed' brass manhole covers placed within granite paving laid out by Plečnik.[4]

Jože Plečnik 1920–34

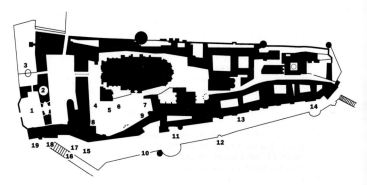

Jože Plečnik 1920–34

Hradčany to Nové Město

The 16.4-metre Mrákotín granite monolith[5] was financed by Masaryk and erected unfinished in 1928 by Plečnik, on the tenth anniversary of the foundation of the Republic. A taller monolith dedicated to the Czech soldiers who died in the First World War was originally intended to be placed on the steps in the Paradise Garden but, much to Plečnik's annoyance, was broken during transportation from the Moravian quarry.

The Gothic statue of St George fighting a dragon was moved to a new position and placed on a pedestal surrounded by water and a circular rail designed by Plečnik.[6] He also adapted the Baroque fountain[7] by the entrance to the old Royal Palace.

On the opposite side of the Courtyard is Plečnik's gateway for the President's car[8] and beyond lies the President's private apartment.

From the fountain turn right to the Bull Staircase with its draped copper canopy.[9] The detailing, the niche decorations, door handles, balustrades and careful arrangement of masonry show Plečnik at his best. The view from the landing aligning Plečnik's pyramid with the Church of St Nicholas is staggering.

In the Ramparts Garden below, a number of elements have been designed and arranged by Plečnik – the Belvedere pavilion[10] and a granite beam beside the Vilém Slavata z Chlumu monument of the 1618 defenestration.[11] Further along, eastwards, is a staircase leading down from the ramparts to the gardens below,[12] the Bellevue pavilion,[13] and almost right at the end is the Moravian Bastion[14] with a 12-metre-high, thin, granite obelisk and a Měřín granite table under a pergola.

From the Ramparts Garden move on to the Paradise Garden,[15] where a powerful and massive Mrákotín granite basin is suspended on two small granite blocks above the well-kept lawn. As you mount the steps[16] do not miss the wall fountain under the stairs on the right, the stone balus-

Jože Plečnik 1920–34

trade, the black diorite vase, the gilded window grille[17] above and the amphora in the niche.[18]

Leave through Plečnik's gate,[19] with its stone balustrade, back on to the square from where you started.

In 1991 the British architect James Stirling visited Prague Castle to give a lecture and was shown Plečnik's architecture. He was so fascinated that he insisted on being photographed at all of Plečnik's works; despite a bomb threat he refused to leave until he had seen everything.

First Courtyard 1920–23
Paradise and Ramparts Gardens 1920–27
President's Apartment 1921–27
Moravian Bastion Obelisk 1923
Bastion Garden 1927–32
Second Courtyard 1927
Third Courtyard 1928–32
Monolith 1928
Plečnik Hall 1928–1930
Bull Staircase and Canopy 1928–32

ADDRESS Pražský hrad, Praha 1 Hradčany
METRO Hradčanská – Line A
TRAM 22
ACCESS open (apart from the Plečnik Hall and Apartment); gardens closed in winter

Hradčany to Nové Město

Jože Plečnik 1920–34

Jože Plečnik 1920–34

Completion of St Vitus Cathedral

St Vitus Cathedral is a microcosm of the architectural history of the city. It has been built over 1000 years and all architectural periods are represented here. The tall 96.6-metre bell tower epitomises this. It began to be built in Gothic times, in 1392, by the German architect Peter Parler, but remained unfinished. Almost 160 years later the tower was completed in the Renaissance style with a rendered brickwork viewing gallery and a copper-covered cupola. The cupola was damaged by lightning in 1760 and replaced in 1770 by a more exuberant three-tier Baroque-shaped edifice giving Prague a distinctive landmark.

The western nave of the Cathedral from the choir to the twin tower elevation is in the neo-Gothic style. It was started in 1873 and finished in 1929. The bronze entrance gates designed by Vratislav H. Brunner and Otakar Španiel (1927–29) show the building of the Cathedral on the central panels and the lives of St Wenceslas and St Adalbert on the side doors. The stained-glass rose west window was designed by František Kysela (1927–29); it depicts scenes from the Creation of the World. Alphonse Mucha's window (1931) can be seen in the Archbishops' Chapel on the north side.

In St Wenceslas Chapel the cast-glass windows looking onto the Third Courtyard are by Stanislav Libenský and Jaroslava Brychtová (1964–69). Even the modern era is not excluded.

ADDRESS Katedrála Sv. Víta, Pražský hrad, Praha 1 Hradčany
METRO Hradčanská – Line A
TRAM 22
ACCESS open 9.00–17.00 daily

Josef Mocker, Kamil Hilbert 1873–1929

Hradčany to Nové Město

Hradčany to Nové Město

Josef Mocker, Kamil Hilbert 1873–1929

Tombs of Czech Kings

Deep under the Cathedral, in a small cave-like crypt, are eight sarcophagi arranged by architect Kamil Roškot between 1934 and 1935. The centre tomb, of King Charles IV (1316–78), is a streamlined design, meticulously styled and crafted in metal, like a shiny science-fiction time machine set into the marble floor, appearing to be ready, vibrating, for a journey into space. It is surrounded by the tombs of other famous Czech kings and personalities. On the right is King Ladislav Pohrobek (1440–57), behind is King Václav IV (1361–1419) with his half brother, Jan Zhořelecký, and Maria Amelia, the daughter of Empress Maria Theresia. On the left is King Jiří z Poděbrad (1420–71), four wives of King Charles IV, and his children. Behind King Charles IV's tomb is the original pewter coffin of King Rudolf II (1552–1612).

ADDRESS Katedrála Sv. Víta, Pražský hrad, Praha 1 Hradčany
METRO Hradčanská – Line A
TRAM 22
ACCESS open 9.00–17.00 daily

Kamil Roškot 1934–35

Kamil Roškot 1934–35

Reconstruction of the Theresian Wing, Prague Castle

During the reign of Empress Maria Theresia (1740–80) Prague Castle was extensively rebuilt. The Castle was badly damaged during the Prussian siege of Prague in 1757 and the task of renovation was given to the Italian architect Nicolo F.L. Pacassi, who enveloped the top of the Hradčany Hill and the courtyards around St Vitus Cathedral with long, plain, French-style, Classical buildings accommodating the royal residence.

After the foundation of the Czechoslovak Republic in 1918, work started at Prague Castle to establish a fitting home for the President from the neglected areas of the old and new Royal Palace. Apart from Plečnik, Otto Rothmayer, his gifted pupil, was commissioned from 1922 until 1951 to renovate parts of the Palace and the attached Theresian Wing. Romanesque and Gothic remains were reinforced and renovated.

Part of the reconstruction consisted of the insertion of a Požáry granite circular staircase leading from the late-Gothic Vladislav Hall, built between 1493 and 1502, on to the terraces and through the Theresian Wing to the gardens below. Rothmayer designed this element with an elegant, thin, fluted copper roof and steel rod and hoop balustrade with gilded connectors, which settled cosily into the historical context of the Castle proving that modern and past architecture can live happily side by side.

ADDRESS Královský palác, Pražský hrad, Praha 1 Hradčany
METRO Hradčanská – Line A
TRAM 22
ACCESS open 9.00–16.30 daily

Hradčany to Nové Město

Otto Rothmayer 1930–51

Hradčany to Nové Město

Otto Rothmayer 1930–51

Orangery

A deep green valley to the north of Prague Castle is all that remains of the castle moat which encircled it and is called Jelení příkop (Deer Moat). Despite the name, bears used to roam its steep slopes in the interwar period. Now the bears have gone and the walk along the edge of the moat is opened where, to the west of Prašný most (Powder Bridge), lies the restored Masaryk's Terrace by Jože Plečnik. To the east of the bridge, against the Renaissance wall surrounding Královská zahrada (Royal Garden) and on a sunny narrow plateau at the moat's edge, is a new orangery by Eva Jiřičná. The orangery, which replaces an existing glasshouse, was built for the cultivation of decorative plants for the castle and it is the first building by Jiřičná in Prague.

In the 16th century orangeries and glasshouses were located here to grow and supply exotic fruit to the castle. The new orangery continues this long tradition and it is a pleasure to see that it truthfully reflects the late 20th century era in which it has been designed. The orangery structure is a shell formed of a diagonal net of stainless-steel tubes from which is suspended a glass skin. This creates a clear, unobstructed semicircular volume divided into three compartments within the orangery's 100-metre length.

This is a refined and appropriate piece of architecture to celebrate Jiřičná's homecoming.

ADDRESS Jelení příkop, Pražský hrad, Praha 1 Hradčany
METRO Hradčanská – Line A
TRAM 22
ACCESS none

Eva Jiřičná 1995–96

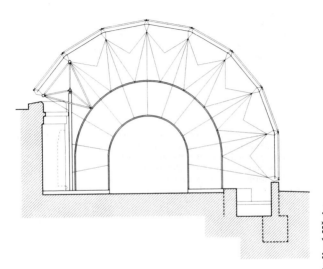

Eva Jiřičná 1995–96

Malostranská Metro Station

The dominant and monumental architecture of most of Prague's metro stations is happily excluded from the treatment of the Malostranská station. The location of copied Baroque sculptures at the exit level gives the metro users a taste of the medieval quarter beyond. The low building, clad in black marble, sits well with the Waldstein Equestrian School, now used as an art gallery, and the neighbouring garden with fountains and water troughs. The modern metalwork gates and grilles inserted into arched openings cast intriguing shadows on the surrounding high walls. The garden is a suitable space for a tranquil break and seclusion from the busy world of tourists and passers-by.

Another notable metro station interior is Karlovo náměstí on Line B where the platform walls are lined with specially pressed, ribbed and shaped glass blocks. The main support pillars are faced on their flat side with glass sheets laminated with aluminium foil giving the whole interior an image of toughness with a permanent sparkle (Lubomír Hanel, Jan Talacko, Miroslav Pelcl, 1985).

Hradčany to Nové Město

ADDRESS Klárov, Praha 1 Malá Strana
METRO Malostranská – Line A
TRAM 12, 18, 22
ACCESS open

Zdeněk Drobný (station) and Otakar Kuča (garden) 1979

Zdeněk Drobný (station) and Otakar Kuča (garden) 1979

Svatopluk Čech Bridge
(most Svatopluka Čecha)

In 1905 Jan Koula won a competition to design a new bridge across the Vltava and skilfully resolved the difficult problem of connecting the two river banks of unequal height. This Prague bridge, named after a Czech writer and poet who lived between 1846 and 1908, is the shortest at 169 metres and is 16 metres wide. The elegant, shallow, light steel structure appears to spring effortlessly from pier to pier. The soft, lacework-like detailing of the balustrades expresses Koula's desire to coordinate the metal into a meaningful composition.

The high Ionic columns, with statues of Victoria (by Antonín Popp), were intended as monumental connecting elements with a triumphant arch framing a deep cutting into the Letná Plain above, which was never realised. Koula's plan was superseded by a tunnel opposite the Šverma Bridge, decided on after numerous competitions. The 429-metre-long tunnel was eventually built between 1949 and 1953.

Above the bridge on the edge of Letná Plain stood a 15-metre-high statue of Stalin, designed by Otakar Švec, erected on a 15-metre-high pedestal, in 1955. It soon became an embarrassment and was removed by explosives in 1962. The caverns remaining under the pedestal were used for storage and graced with sacks of rotting potatoes. The pedestal is currently a site for a Metronome sculpture by Vratislav K. Novák (1991), which measures the new democratic time, its long wagging finger reminding Prague to avoid further follies in the future.

ADDRESS continuation of Pařížská, Praha 1 Staré Město
METRO Staroměstská – Line A
TRAM 12, 17
ACCESS open

Jan Koula and Jiří Soukup (engineering) 1905–08

Jan Koula and Jiří Soukup (engineering) 1905–08

Memorial to the Victims of Communism

While standing on the Svatopluk Čech Bridge look up at the steep slope leading to the Letná Plain. There Future Systems want to locate a memorial to the victims of Communism – a permanent scar carved into the natural setting. A cut would be made into the hill with a stainless-steel lightweight bridge suspended between the sloping side walls, rising in 42 steps symbolising the number of years of the Communist regime. The walls would be faced in black glass and inscribed with the names of all the innocent who lost their lives. A fitting and appropriate tribute to those who died on the gallows, in prisons, in police and secret-service custody, in labour camps and uranium mines and while illegally crossing the country borders. This project lies particularly close to my heart as my father, Rudolf Margolius, was one of the eleven men unlawfully executed in December 1952 as a result of the infamous Slánský Trial.

Not surprisingly the current political climate is too sensitive and volatile to such an open and permanent display of the errors of the recent past and the construction of this profound and moving project so elegantly envisaged seems, at least at the moment, unlikely.

ADDRESS south face of Letná Hill
in line with Svatopluk Čech Bridge,
Praha 1 Staré Město
METRO Staroměstská – Line A
TRAM 12, 17
ACCESS unrealised project

Future Systems: Jan Kaplický and Amanda Levete 1993

Future Systems: Jan Kaplický and Amanda Levete 1993

Cooperative Housing

This block of Cubist apartment buildings was built for a Teachers' Cooperative Society after the end of the First World War. The buildings were designed comparatively late in the Cubist period and were not directly affected by the power of French Cubist painters. The soft, subtle modelling with strong colour variations used for external finishes is surprising for a Cubist architectural composition, usually finished in a single colour. The influence of the later, more colourful Rondo-Cubist style is detectable.

Every element was considered in the skilful symmetrical design including window frames, entrance gates and doors. From a distance one appreciates the tall, tiled roof which appears to be too heavy and in sharp contrast to the fragile, origami-like façade.

Hradčany to Nové Město

ADDRESS Elišky Krásnohorské 10–14 / 123, 1021, 1037, Praha 1 Staré Město
METRO Staroměstská – Line A
TRAM 17
ACCESS none

Otakar Novotný 1919–21

Hradčany to Nové Město

Office Building, Liliová

Tucked away deep in the courtyard of an old Renaissance house, 'At the Golden Chair', one can find this surprisingly fresh, high-tech refurbishment and extension expressing itself most clearly in the new lift and stair tower. At night it glows, accentuating a framework of green steel structure with red diagonal bracing. Holes cut into the external structure are projected onto the white walls and dance among the shadows.

The rear part of the courtyard was built in the 1920s on top of a one-storey building. In the corner there used to be a small service block which was demolished to make way for the new vertical lift and stair shaft. The outside wall of the tower is angled away from the floor line, creating triangular openings, glazed in heavy glass, allowing light to filter through the floors and lighten the enclosure. The effect is reinforced by the glass envelope around the lift shaft and the use of glass blocks and ribbed sheet glass for internal walls.

ADDRESS Liliová 4 / 250, Praha 1 Staré Město
METRO Staroměstská – Line A
TRAM 17, 18
ACCESS none

Jaroslav Šafer 1992

Hradčany to Nové Město

Jaroslav Šafer 1992

Štenc House

A building designed for a fine-arts publisher, Jan Štenc (1871–1947). The architect, Otakar Novotný, was Kotěra's student and was influenced by the works of the Dutch architect Hendrik Petrus Berlage, and by Frank Lloyd Wright. This is clearly evident in the Štenc House. It is placed in a dark corner of the little square and crowded by the evangelical Renaissance St Salvator Church with Baroque alterations.

The use of exposed brickwork externally and internally is, in itself, unusual in Bohemia. Red bricks, white glazed bricks and small granite sets are arranged in a strong, rational composition with little hint of decoration. A surprisingly heavy, rounded brick balcony projects out of the otherwise unmodulated façade. Large glass panels and windows facing the internal, brick-paved courtyard and the glazed, curved roof on the street elevation heralded very early the coming of the new architectural era.

ADDRESS Salvátorská 8–10 / 931, 1092,
Praha 1 Staré Město
METRO Staroměstská – Line A
TRAM 17, 18
ACCESS none

Otakar Novotný 1909–11

Otakar Novotný 1909–11

Extension to Charles University

A daring piece of modern architectural infill in a very sensitive area. In this part of Prague several Gothic houses were taken over by Charles University, including the large Rotlev House given to the University by King Václav IV in 1383. These buildings were reconstructed a number of times, most recently between 1711 and 1718 by František M. Kaňka.

In the late 1940s and 1950s renovation was carried out so that the buildings could fill the contemporary educational requirements of the university. At the same time, a new building was designed to be squeezed between the historical houses and to accommodate the chancellor's offices and administration. The smooth red brickwork rectangle with well-proportioned windows is held down by an oversailing canopy-like roof. The small architectural elements, the paving, fence enclosure and flagpoles, add dignity to the serene surroundings.

ADDRESS Ovocný trh 3, Praha 1 Staré Město
METRO Můstek – Lines A and B
ACCESS open

Jaroslav Fragner 1946–69

Jaroslav Fragner 1946–69

'At the Black Madonna' Department Store

An attractive corner position, almost at the end of Celetná and the turning to Ovocný trh (previously the Fruit Market) which is terminated by the recently renovated Stavovské (Estates) Theatre. This building, designed for František Herbst, is another Cubist creation so particular and appropriate to Prague, a city which seems to have inspired the bizarre and extraordinary. In those days, when architects cooperated closely with artists, writers and poets, their motivation was fuelled by heated discussions, polemics and critiques. Richer architectural output, directly influenced by other artistic branches, was realised in comparison with present times where each artistic arena is closed and guarded from penetration by other muses.

The dark orange façade, gently angled on the centre line, crowned with heavy dormers set in a two-tier clay-tiled Mansard roof, reflects the Baroque and Classical architecture of the surrounding area. The reinforced concrete structure allowed horizontal bands of windows, interrupted only by slim columns, to divide the building clearly into each storey. The shadows play an important role, filling the overhangs and recesses and emphasising the composition's three-dimensional quality.

The building, recently restored, is occupied by the Czech Museum of Fine Arts. A permanent collection of Czech Cubist art is displayed on the fourth and fifth levels. The first-floor café as originally installed has not been put back and the basement bar is a disappointment.

ADDRESS Ovocný trh 19 / 569, Praha 1 Staré Město
METRO Náměstí Republiky – Line B
TRAM 5, 14, 26
ACCESS open Tuesday to Sunday 10.00–18.00

Josef Gočár 1911–12

Hradčany to Nové Město

Josef Gočár 1911–12

Municipal House (Obecní dům)

A large, diamond-shaped site filled to the brim with an exuberant and unusual Secessionist building contains a restaurant, café, wine bar, games and billiard rooms, concert and dance halls, meeting rooms and exhibition galleries. It was built to serve as a centre for Prague's cultural and social life. The exterior is almost too rich to comprehend in one glance. Step by step investigation is needed to take in all the craftsmanship.

Above the entrance are two lampholders by Karel Novák. Higher up is a concave gable mosaic depicting an allegory of Prague Life, designed by Karel Špillar. On either side of the gable are the sculptures Humiliation and Rebirth of the Nation, by Ladislav Šaloun. Many more statues decorate the other façades.

Inside, the most impressive space is the large Smetana Concert Hall capable of accommodating an audience of 1500 people. Leading Czech artists and sculptors contributed their work, decorating the interior of the building, including Alphonse Mucha (City Mayor's Hall), Mikoláš Aleš (wine bar in the basement), Bohumil Kafka (entrance foyer), Josef V. Myslbek and Jan Preisler (Palacký Hall), Max Švabinský (Rieger Hall), and Ladislav Šaloun (Smetana Concert Hall).

Sleepy during the day, the building comes alive after sunset. The architectural elements, detailing, glass screens, the shiny metalwork of brass clocks and heavy chandeliers suspended from the tall ceilings over the velvet seats, multiply indefinitely in long wall mirrors among the cigarette smoke and the aroma of Turkish coffee.

ADDRESS Náměstí Republiky 5 / 1090, Praha 1 Staré Město
METRO Náměstí Republiky – Line B
TRAM 5, 14, 26
ACCESS open

Hradčany to Nové Město

Antonín Balšánek and Osvald Polívka 1905–12

Antonín Balšánek and Osvald Polívka 1905–12

'At the God's Eye' House

Another skilful and sensitive courtyard development of a medieval residential building can be found in this quiet part of Prague under the shadow of the celebrated Baroque Church of St Jacob.

The original house, U božího oka, was built for Viktorin Křinecký z Ronova in 1501. The new work by Kordovský provides extended office accommodation stretching from the existing building into the courtyard. The new external façade of the extension is layered with clear varnished timber louvres bringing the required shading and privacy to the offices as well as softening the harder cladding materials hidden beyond. The oval toilet block is unusually treated with copper cladding, creating a hard sculptural element that offers a contrast of forms, materials and colours.

Similar, but in a clear Deconstructivist vein with a touch of Japanese flavour, is the courtyard scheme at Mikulandská 12 / 118, Praha 1 Nové Město by Atelier 8000 (Martin Krupauer and Jiří Střítecký) from 1994 to 1995.

ADDRESS Malá Štupartská 7 / 634 and 9 / 1028, Praha 1 Staré Město
METRO Náměstí Republiky – Line B
TRAM 5, 14, 26
ACCESS none

Petr Kordovský 1994

Hradčany to Nové Město

Petr Kordovský 1994

Merkur Palace

Originally built for the Merkur Insurance Company, more recently this building was taken over by Czechoslovak Airlines as their city terminal for transport to and from Prague's Ruzyně Airport. Airport coaches still regularly depart from Řásnovka, the cheapest way to get there from the city centre.

Merkur's short, north elevation faces onto the Vltava embankment terminating the long block of buildings along Revoluční třída. It is a strong Functionalist building, clad in stone of heavy proportions and grey colour giving the whole composition a severe expression, coldness and awkwardness not usually associated with designs from the same period.

ADDRESS Revoluční 25 / 767, Praha 1 Staré Město
METRO Náměstí Republiky – Line B
TRAM 5, 14, 26
ACCESS ground floor open

Jaroslav Fragner 1934–35

Jaroslav Fragner 1934–35

Hradčany to Nové Město

Bílá Labuť Department Store

A department store designed for the Brouk and Babka company. The street elevation has a Thermolux glass wall of 30 by 20 metres supported by a light, steel framework. Daylight enters the deep shopping space through the floor to ceiling glass façade, giving the building a distinctive look and attracting shoppers during evening hours, when it is illuminated from within.

When built, Bílá Labuť (White Swan) was well equipped with heating, mechanical ventilation and air-conditioning, and with special systems for advertising and pneumatic post. Goods were transported by lifts, paternosters and conveyors. For customers' use there were five ten-person lifts. In addition, there was a lift for the offices and an escalator with a capacity of 4000 people per hour.

Presently all these elements are in need of renovation in order to bring this interesting shopping emporium up-to-date with the latest requirements for selling, display and the comfort of shoppers. One hopes it will soon be full of good-quality, Czech-manufactured goods.

ADDRESS Na poříčí 23 / 1068, Praha 1 Nové Město
METRO Náměstí Republiky – Line B
TRAM 3, 24
ACCESS open Monday to Friday 8.30–19.00, Saturday 9.00–16.00

Josef Kittrich and Josef Hrubý, interiors by Jan Gillar 1937–39

Josef Kittrich and Josef Hrubý, interiors by Jan Gillar 1937–39

Bank of the Czechoslovak Legions

Four main columns, from ground to first floor, support four sculptural figures depicting scenes from the life and battles of the Czech legions by Jan Štursa: The Legion in the Trenches, Defiance and Courage, Waiting and Yearning for Home, The Throwing Grenades and Defence against Gas. The horizontal bas relief above, by Otto Gutfreund, shows The Legionnaires' Homecoming.

The style of this late-Cubist building is known as Rondo-Cubism in Bohemia. This architectural trend was influenced by Czech folklore motifs and possibly by Fernand Léger's style of painting which used circular forms as a development of Cubist painting.

Circular forms are taken through the whole building. The façade is crowned by a monumental, cantilevered cornice and punctuated by windows and heavy circular granite forms. Inside, the form of the main banking hall, with its glazed roof, though of heavier structure, is reminiscent of Otto Wagner's Post Office Savings Bank in Vienna and is rich with round and military motifs which cover the floors, walls, screens, grilles and even the door leaves, all made in expensive and impressive materials.

The bank was criticised after its completion by architect Oldřich Starý as 'reflecting the chaos of contemporary time', emphasising the uncertainty about which direction architectural development would take.

ADDRESS Na poříčí 24 / 1046, Praha 1 Nové Město
METRO Náměstí Republiky – Line B
TRAM 3, 24
ACCESS ground floor open

Josef Gočár 1921–23

Assicurazioni Generali & Moldavia Generali Building and Broadway Arcade

The centre of Prague has many passageways, shopping arcades, inner courtyards and parks enclosed by street-facing façades. To utilise plots to their full the block interiors were built over rather than used as gardens and this has resulted in a tight urban pattern. If you do not know where these arcades are the only way to find them is to venture into each large doorway and make your own discoveries.

One of these is the Broadway which runs from Na příkopě to Celetná and contains a few tiny shops, offices and a cinema situated in the basement. The street elevations, clad in travertine, are rather plain. The real drama is enacted in the arcade by the bold roof structures. A popular treatment was to set the glass blocks in a reinforced concrete frame and many different alternatives were employed. The two successive roofs of the Broadway are impressive, particularly because of their irregular plan shape and the way the glass blocks are supported and follow the form of the frame.

On leaving, note the stainless steel gates which are hinged horizontally at high level. Late at night they are lowered to secure the interior.

ADDRESS Na příkopě 31 / 988, Praha 1 Staré Město
METRO Náměstí Republiky – Line B
TRAM 5, 14, 26
ACCESS arcade open

Bohumír Kozák and Antonín Černý 1936–38

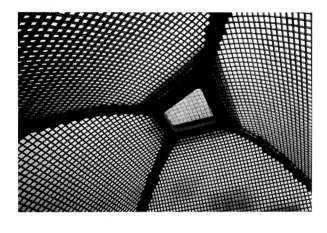

Hradčany to Nové Město

Bohumír Kozák and Antonín Černý 1936–38

Myslbek Development

Myslbek is a large commercial development whose beginning has been clouded by heated debate. The tender for the site, which had remained empty since 1926 when the Union Bank had it cleared for a new building, was won by a French bank, Caisse des Depots et Consignations. The bank appointed Claude Parent as its architect and, after a local competition, his Czech collaborators were chosen. The City of Prague has a 20 per cent stake in this multifunction building with three carpark basement levels, three shopping levels and six floors of offices. A controversial carpark ramp starts at Panská Street and emerges at Ovocný trh.

The development stands on the site of the ancient city walls and the pedestrian passageway through the building symbolically recreates a wall with a gateway between the modern Na příkopě and the medieval Ovocný trh. The architectural expression is unclear as it attempts to embrace too many international and local themes in response to the various neighbouring styles as well as current architectural fashion. The gateway facing north-east is distorted, as are the roof dormers, perhaps inspired by Gočár's Cubist house nearby. On the Na příkopě façade the applied diagonal motif symbolising a gate, which is open by day and closed at night, only adds to the confusion of the concept.

ADDRESS Na příkopě, Praha 1 Nové Město
METRO Můstek – Lines A and B
ACCESS shopping levels and passageway open

Claude Parent with Zdeněk Hölzel and Jan Kerel 1992–96

Claude Parent with Zdeněk Hölzel and Jan Kerel 1992–96

Bondy Department Store and Černá Růže Arcade

This L-shaped arcade is much larger than the Broadway Arcade. It has an indoor exhibition space and market. The modern building infill faces into Panská Street which is connected, with the arcade, to the neo-Renaissance house 'At the Black Rose', built in 1847 by Jan D. Frenzl at Na příkopě 12 / 853.

The shallow, arched, glazed roof formed from round Luxfer glass blocks inserted into a reinforced concrete structure daringly spans the arcade. This attractive construction idea was used here for the first time. The surrounding galleries have floors in glass block to allow maximum light to reach the ground floor. The original suspended and standard column globe light fittings have unfortunately been removed but the 1930s' aura is still detectable. The unsuitable central stairs to the upper levels were inserted in 1960.

The second smaller arcade associated with the Panská building has an external glass vertical wall with staircase and glass-framed lift allowing additional light into the interior.

ADDRESS Panská 4 / 894, Praha 1 Nové Město
METRO Můstek – Lines A and B
TRAM 3, 9, 14, 24
ACCESS arcade open

Oldřich Tyl 1929–33

Oldřich Tyl 1929–33

Department Store, Provaznická

A white rendered building, located in a narrow street away from the bustle of the busy shopping street Na příkopě, peers out with its projected round corner towards the promenade to attract passers-by.

With the sun on its white façade it stands out clearly and those interested in architecture are drawn closer to inspect this little jewel.

ADDRESS Provaznická 13 / 397, Praha 1 Staré Město
METRO Můstek – Lines A and B
ACCESS none

Adolf Foehr 1930–32

Adolf Foehr 1930–32

ČKD Building

An office and administration building designed for a large industrial conglomerate, Českomoravská Kolben Daněk, whose production base is located in Prague 9, Vysočany. It is a building with a modern concept, attempting to balance the strong neighbouring stores and palaces on Wenceslas Square. Clad in granite with stainless-steel framing to three protruding windows, this corner building has a bar and disco on the roof terrace blaring out music while laser beams sweep over the night sky above the square. The ground floor of the block is largely open, accommodating an entrance to the Můstek metro station, a small café and a shop.

The architects used a clock to terminate the building against the skyline similar to the 1930s-style ARA Department Store further down the street in Perlová. They placed it asymmetrically to give visual support to the neighbouring Viennese Union Bank building designed by Josef Zasche between 1906 and 1908. It is a pity that the ČKD Building is not more modest and lower, allowing a better view of the Old Town beyond.

ADDRESS Na příkopě 1 / 388, Praha 1 Staré Město
METRO Můstek – Lines A and B
ACCESS ground and top floors open

Alena Šrámková and Jan Šrámek 1978–83

Alena Šrámková and Jan Šrámek 1978–83

ARA Department Store

A typical sleek white Functionalist design built for the textile merchant, Amschelberg, for the sale of fabrics and fashion. The original project was designed by Milan Babuška and later reworked by František Řehák.

The steel structure of the building, one of the first constructed in this way in Prague, allowed slender façade elements and the suspension of the curved corner from the top floors to free the pavement from vertical supports. This space was recently utilised by introducing another Můstek metro entrance. Its curved soaring tower and square clock complements the corner of this urban space and is a good opposite to the exuberant Adriatica Palace. Long vistas from Jungmannova are well terminated by the verticality of the architecture shooting up to the sky.

ADDRESS Perlová 5 / 371, Praha 1 Staré Město
METRO Můstek – Lines A and B
ACCESS ground floor open

František Řehák and Milan Babuška 1927–31

František Řehák and Milan Babuška 1927–31

Retail and Apartment Building, Jungmannovo náměstí

This is one of the first Rondo-Cubist buildings built in Prague. Round, colour motifs were used in opposition to the grey and white sharp diagonal and pyramidal forms of pure Cubism. Both elevations, to 28. října and Jungmannovo náměstí, set up a pattern for the most popular colour combination of red and white, the Czech national colours.

The enthusiasm for a connection with folklore stemmed from the foundation of the Czechoslovak Republic in 1918, and the spirit of the new independent country, with its Slavonic language and culture, was imprinted and celebrated in art and architecture.

This is a narrow building, but with heavily formed coloured bands and a rounded balcony and gable it makes its mark, particularly along the sunny square, and cannot be missed by any observant visitor to the city.

ADDRESS Jungmannovo náměstí 4 / 764, Praha 1 Nové Město
METRO Můstek – Lines A and B
TRAM 6, 9, 18, 22
ACCESS ground floor open

Rudolf Stockar 1920–22

Rudolf Stockar 1920–22

Music Store

Jungmannovo náměstí is a small and magical square containing several architectural masterpieces: Stockar's retail and apartment building, a Cubist lamp post, Janák's Adriatica Palace and a second Adriatica building on the corner at Jungmannova 34 / 750 which was designed by Fritz Lehmann and Kamil Roškot (1929–31). In the late 1930s an elegant four-level music store was built in the square. The simple but attractive building supplements the broad variety of architectural styles and sits comfortably attached to the tall wall surrounding the Gothic church of Our Lady of the Snow with its nave completed in 1606 during the Renaissance period.

ADDRESS Jungmannovo náměstí 17 / 754, Praha 1 Nové Město
METRO Můstek – Lines A and B
TRAM 6, 9, 18, 22
ACCESS all levels open

Vlastimil Brožek, Jan Mentberger, Karel Polívka 1938–39

Hradčany to Nové Město

Vlastimil Brožek, Jan Mentberger, Karel Polívka 1938–39

Riunione Adriatica di Sicurta Palace

This is a rich wedding cake of Renaissance proportions, a very unusual slant of late Cubism with extravagantly detailed façades, including sculptural decorations by Otto Gutfreund and Jan Štursa's Seafaring statue placed on the cornice of the Národní elevation. The interiors are rich and colourful, particularly the ground-floor passageway and entrance.

There is no precedent or follower to this architecture in Prague and it is hard to understand where the inspiration came from. Yet Adriatica seems to sit quite happily on the corner of Jungmannova and Národní, in sharp contrast to the smooth white ara building on the opposite side, adding variety and interest to the street atmosphere.

ADDRESS Jungmannova 3 1 / 36,
Praha 1 Nové Město
METRO Můstek – Lines A and B
TRAM 6, 9, 18, 22
ACCESS ground floor, first-floor
restaurant and terrace open

Pavel Janák and Josef Zasche 1922–25

Škoda Works Administrative Building

It is interesting to see and compare two adjoining buildings which came to life from the hands of the same architect. The Škoda Works Building was designed a year after the Adriatica, but what a difference between the two. The unusual Rondo-Cubist motifs were replaced by stronger cubic shapes projected regularly out of the façade, contrasting with the recessed windows, to create a three-dimensional grid emphasised by mass, light and shadow. At the top of the building there was originally a sculptural relief of the Škoda winged arrow trademark designed and sculpted by Otto Gutfreund.

The rectilinear forms of the Škoda elevation play against the more floral Adriatica elements, one building fighting the other for supremacy, but the result of the contest is a definite draw.

ADDRESS Jungmannova 29 / 747,
Praha 1 Nové Město
METRO Můstek – Lines A and B
TRAM 6, 9, 18, 22
ACCESS none

Hradčany to Nové Město

Pavel Janák 1923–26

Pavel Janák 1923–26

Urbánek House

An unusual building, designed for a music and arts publisher, Mojmír Urbánek, containing a shop, small concert hall – the Mozarteum – offices on the first floor and apartments on the upper floors. A deep frame borders the whole composition and is terminated by a large triangular gable. The front elevation has a subtle graduation, storey by storey, as the surrounding brickwork planes around windows recess further into the house. The full-height border framing remains, building up its thickness and complexity as it rises towards the gable. It appears as if the elevation consisted of sliding planes fitting into side grooves like giant four-pane sash windows. Such treatment produces animation of the design.

The base of the façade is decorated with two sculptures by Jan Štursa supporting a large horizontal window to the offices running across the whole elevation. Kotěra avoided the Cubist style but its influence can be perceived in the use of protruding windows and the detailing of metalwork.

ADDRESS Jungmannova 30 / 748, Praha 1 Nové Město
METRO Můstek – Lines A and B
TRAM 6, 9, 18, 22
ACCESS ground floor open

Jan Kotěra 1912–13

Jan Kotěra 1912–13

Koruna Palace

Wenceslas Square is, in itself, an architectural gallery. Almost every building along its 682-metre length is of interest. A number of buildings from very different periods sit comfortably together, watched over from the top by Josef Václav Myslbek's statue of St Wenceslas accompanied by four Czech patron saints, gradually placed there between 1912 and 1924.

The Koruna Palace, named after the Koruna (Crown) Insurance Company for which the building was designed, is a well-composed late-Secession-inspired building yet, in other aspects, it looks ahead to a more advanced era. The Secession period can be seen in its decoration and sculptural motifs at upper levels in contrast to the treatment of the lower part, with an exposed simple structural frame and large glass infill panels and windows. The tower statues, supporting the stylised crown, are by Vojtěch Sucharda. The Palace stands on the site of U Špinků House where a Viennese-type café, the first in Prague, was situated and frequented by leading Czech politicians in the 1860s. The tall square tower, placed unusually off the corner, emulates the position of the tower on the original old building.

Next to the Na příkopě side of Koruna Palace a small store called Adam (previously Kníže) designed in the 1930s by Heinrich Kulka, Adolf Loos's pupil, was carefully restored with a new shop front installed by ADNS (Václav Alda, Petr Dvořák, Martin Němec, Jan Stempel, 1992).

ADDRESS Václavské náměstí 1 / 846, Praha 1 Nové Město
METRO Můstek – Lines A and B
TRAM 3, 9, 14, 24
ACCESS ground floor open

Antonín Pfeiffer 1911–14

Hradčany to Nové Město

Antonín Pfeiffer 1911–14

Lindt Department Store

One of the first avant-garde department store buildings in Prague, conceived in a pioneering style. The Lindt Department Store came about as a clear solution to the client's requirements. It is built of reinforced concrete on a rational structural grid. The vertical circulation is resolved simply by lifts and stairs positioned centrally on the party wall and a ground-floor passageway provides a link to Jungmann Square allowing good public contact with the building.

What used to be the curved glazing, now replaced by metal sheets, at the top of the main elevation softens the height of the store. However, the opaque black glass cladding to the floor zones in combination with the dark large upper-level continuous windows is detrimental to the building's final impact, especially late in the evening when it disappears altogether.

ADDRESS Václavské náměstí 4 / 773,
Praha 1 Nové Město
METRO Můstek – Lines A and B
TRAM 3, 9, 14, 24
ACCESS ground floor open

Ludvík Kysela 1925–27

Ludvík Kysela 1925–27

Lamp Post

The best way to find this interesting architectural element is to pass from Wenceslas Square along the passageway in Lindt House and turn left. There you will find a lamp post. The juxtaposition of this Cubist street furniture with the Gothic gateway and its triangular gable (1360–80), leading to the graveyard of the Church of Our Lady of the Snow, the Functionalist Baťa Building and the late Secession-Cubist Adam Pharmacy Building is typical Prague scenery – the comfortable combination and mingling of styles.

The Adam Pharmacy Building (1911–13) with its main façade facing Wenceslas Square 8 / 775 is also by Emil Králíček and Matěj Blecha and has notable and fine details. The statues of Adam and Eve on the front elevation are by Karel Pavlík and Antonín Odehnal. The rear of the building echoes more strongly the Cubist style of the lamp post.

The authorship of the lamp post was, in the past, subscribed to the architect Vlastislav Hofman.

ADDRESS Jungmannovo náměstí,
Praha 1, Nové Město
METRO Můstek – Lines A and B
ACCESS open

Emil Králíček and Matěj Blecha 1912

Baťa Department Store

A purpose-built store for Tomáš Baťa (1876–1932), the famous founder of the shoe empire. Baťa's fully automated manufacture was based in the town of Zlín in Moravia. He encouraged an avant-garde approach both to shoe manufacture and architecture, producing, displaying and selling his goods as well as housing his employees in the most up-to-date accommodation. By the early 1930s, Baťa owned 45 buildings and had 16,000 employees producing 150,000 pairs of shoes a day! The department store was designed for the sole purpose of selling Baťa footware. Each storey was linked by lifts and side staircases and had minimum corridors in the sales areas. The main staircase has now been replaced by escalators. The structure is a reinforced concrete frame, whose columns are filled with cast iron and have the smallest possible cross section, identical in each storey. The front and back elevations are almost alike and fully clad in glass. Between the continuous bands of windows thin floor slab zones are covered with translucent white glass, which were used for advertising. The same glass also frames the façade vertically on each side.

The recent (1990–92) restoration and cladding replacement revealed the rational structure of the floor plates. The entrance in the Lindt Store passageway was closed off, rather robbing this busy space of additional attraction. The original tubular steel furniture and fittings were substituted by rather limp 1990s imitations.

The building should not be missed in the evening when it glows with light, a giant advert for Baťa shoes and heroic Functionalist architecture.

ADDRESS Václavské náměstí 6 / 774, Praha 1 Nové Město
METRO Můstek – Lines a and b
TRAM 3, 9, 14, 24
ACCESS open

Ludvík Kysela and Baťa Project Office 1927–29

Peterka Department Store

In the Peterka Store, Jan Kotěra, the founder of Czech modern architecture, has produced a subtle and soft Secession composition. The façade is composed of three vertical elements, two higher book-end pieces gently squeezing the central bay, which supports the sculptural relief by Josef Pekárek and Karel Novák. Varied metal balcony railings add texture to the closely modern composition. The decoration of Secessionist plant motifs above the first floor enhances the design. The elegant treatment of the lower storeys, accommodating an entrance and shop windows, set up a standard for future designers.

ADDRESS Václavské náměstí 12 / 777, Praha 1 Nové Město
METRO Můstek – Lines A and B
TRAM 3, 9, 14, 24
ACCESS ground floor open

Jan Kotěra 1899–1900

Jan Kotěra 1899–1900

Hradčany to Nové Město

Hotel Juliš

This is an impressive building and its proportions are well conceived. It is based on a typical Prague hotel arrangement with a cinema in the basement, a patisserie on the ground floor, a café on the first floor and the hotel accommodation above. Janák opened up the café interior by means of a large window, probably the biggest of its time, looking out towards Wenceslas Square with its busy traffic and lively atmosphere.

The façade is constructed of steel and glass. The client wanted it to be rich in colour, based on Janák's Rondo-Cubist scheme, from 1920, of the original ground-floor café. However, this time Janák persuaded Karel Juliš to accept a simpler colour scheme. The white translucent Opaxit glass with background lighting, the blue painted steel framing and red metal and neon signs proved to be the only combination which provided impressive night illumination (similar to the Baťa Department Store) and was also attractive during the day.

ADDRESS Václavské náměstí 22 / 782, Praha 1 Nové Město
METRO Můstek – Lines A and B
TRAM 3, 9, 14, 24
ACCESS open

Pavel Janák 1928–33

Pavel Janák 1928–33

U Stýblů Building and Alfa Arcade

A large office building with shops, an arcade and cinema at ground and basement levels. It accommodates another of Prague's arcades with an attractive glass block roof, set in a reinforced concrete frame, this time regular and symmetrical.

The façade to Wenceslas Square has two continuous large vertical square bays topped with glass lean-to structures, the trademark of the building, which contrasts with Kysela's other creations, the rectilinear top of the Baťa building and the rolled glass edge of the Lindt Store. It is a pity that advertising signs have been fitted across the bays, disrupting the clean lines of the façade.

ADDRESS Václavské náměstí 28 / 785, Praha 1 Nové Město
METRO Můstek – Lines A and B
TRAM 3, 9, 14, 24
ACCESS arcade open

Ludvík Kysela and Jan Jarolím 1927–29

Ludvík Kysela and Jan Jarolím 1927–29

Grand Hotel Evropa and Hotel Meran

These two adjacent hotels are the best-preserved Secession-style buildings in Prague. The asymmetrical composition of the two façades is richly decorated with statues holding gold plate and brass lanterns and glazed tiles forming pretty Secessionist floral patterns. All the details, including the signs, are of the right period.

It is best to appreciate the Grand Evropa at leisure, sitting inside the sumptuous restaurant or in a ground-floor or gallery-level café, listening to the piano and observing the wonderful details of the inlaid timber panelling, mosaics and colourful symbolic pictures, the extravagant light fittings and the wealth of brass railings and metalwork.

Bedřich Bendelmayer and Alois Dryák together with Bedřich Ohmann also designed the Secessionist Hotel Central in Hybernská 10 / 1001, Praha 1 Nové Město (1899–1901) which is worth visiting.

ADDRESS Václavské náměstí 25–27 / 865–825, Praha 1 Nové Město
METRO Museum – Lines A and C
TRAM 3, 9, 14, 24
ACCESS open

Bendelmayer, Letzl, Hypšman (Evropa); Dryák (Meran) 1903–05

Moravian Bank

A dominant corner of Wenceslas Square consisting of three large houses with rich façades combining strong horizontal and vertical elements topped with an exquisitely detailed copper-covered roof with inserted shaped windows. This building was built by Matěj Blecha, but it is possible that Emil Králíček was also involved as the designer. The corner is crowned by an extraordinary sculptural hat appearing like the head of a robot (a word, incidentally, invented by the Czech artist and writer Josef Čapek and used by his brother, the writer Karel Čapek in his play *Rossum's Universal Robots*, 1920). Decorative flower and lion motifs and a row of warrior heads with copper helmets line the façades.

When it was finished, this exuberant architecture was misunderstood and attacked by architect Otakar Novotný who called it 'an architectural monster, a colossus of pompous mannerism'.

ADDRESS Václavské náměstí 38–40 / 794–795,
Štěpánská 63 / 626,
Praha 1 Nové Město
METRO Můstek – Lines A and B
TRAM 3, 9, 14, 24
ACCESS ground floor open

Matěj Blecha 1913–16

Matěj Blecha 1913–16

Hradčany to Nové Město

Edison Transformer

In its setting on the edge of a small park surrounded by trees, there is a Japanese feeling to this simply designed building. Zdeněk Pešánek's Světelná kinetická plastika (Luminous Kinetic Sculpture) of white metal and glass elements, its movement controlled by a perforated strip of paper storing information on the sequence of events, came alive at night and was placed on the roof of the single-storey structure above the large doors in 1930.

Unfortunately this sculpture is now lost. Pešánek (1896–1965), a member of Devětsil, was the first artist to use neon light in art. It would be interesting to recreate this piece of avant-garde art to proclaim again the building's function as a house of electricity.

ADDRESS Jeruzalemská 2 / 1321, Praha 1
Nové Město
METRO Hlavní nádraží – Line C
TRAM 3, 9, 14, 24
ACCESS none

František A. Libra 1926–30

František A. Libra 1926–30

Brno Bank

The Brno Bank is similar in appearance to Stockar's Retail and Apartment Building in Jungmann Square but much larger. Here Gočár co-operated with sculptor Karel Dvořák (1893–1950) to create a rather subdued Rondo-Cubist building. Circular motifs are reinforced by the curved corner to Panská and weighted down by the heavy top and the use of dark colours.

A solid and massive building, the bank sits comfortably on the junction of two streets providing a recognisable point in Prague's urban landscape.

Hradčany to Nové Město

ADDRESS Jindrišská 15 / 1308, Praha 1 Nové Město
METRO Můstek – Lines A and B
TRAM 3, 9, 14, 24
ACCESS ground floor open

Josef Gočár 1921–23

Josef Gočár 1921–23

Habich Building

A long building divided horizontally into three zones – ground-floor retail area, three floors of offices, and then three floors of apartments, the top floor with small flats, offices and studios. The rear internal courtyard was used as a car park. It is a reinforced concrete frame construction with Isostone blockwork infill, rendered externally. Interesting contrast is displayed on the façade between the different accommodation elements and the stacking of apartments with balconies creating a play of mass with recesses and projections.

In a similar fashion to Krejcar's Olympic Building, Havlíček intended to display signs on the Habich fixed on the solid bands of the façade between the office floors, celebrating Devětsil's aim of using colourful and neon graphics to affect the urban environment. This 'poetry of advertisements' has long gone and its absence robs the building of another dimension.

ADDRESS Štěpánská 33 / 645, Praha 1 Nové Město
metro Museum – Lines A and C
TRAM 3, 9, 14, 24
ACCESS none

Josef Havlíček and Jaroslav Polívka 1927–28

Josef Havlíček and Jaroslav Polívka 1927–28

Apartment Buildings and Arcade

A Functionalist building with a walk-through arcade at ground level, it was erected in place of an old house, U Hřebeckých (1381), which also had a passageway leading through it. Some insensitive alterations have been made to the arcade, including the part-removal of a glass-block vaulted roof and its replacement with modern plastic rooflights. However, the rounded chromed steel-edge wall showcases remain, as well as the impressive glass balustrade and the popular glass lift enclosure in the entrance foyer to the apartments situated at the upper levels.

ADDRESS Štěpánská 36 / 622 leading to Ve Smečkách 27 / 1920, Praha 1 Nové Město
METRO Museum – Lines A and C
TRAM 3, 9, 14, 24
ACCESS arcade open

Eugene Rosenberg 1937–38

Eugene Rosenberg 1937–38

Lucerna Palace

One of the first reinforced concrete frame structures in Prague, externally reminiscent of Auguste Perret's 25 bis Rue Franklin (1903) in Paris. Lucerna is a large, complex building with seven over-ground and four basement levels accommodating shops, cinema, dance hall, offices, apartments and studios in the upper floors. Below are wine bars and a large hall.

At street level, this building has a shopping arcade which meanders through the block branching in several directions into Štěpánská, V jámě and Wenceslas Square, connecting with other arcades. Sunlight filtering through the glass dome brightens the surviving contemporary metal and glass detailing of the shopfronts and the richly finished marble walls and floors.

Lucerna was built by Václav Havel (1861–1921), grandfather of the popular Czech President.

ADDRESS Vodičkova 36 / 704, Praha 1 Nové Město
METRO Můstek – Lines A and B
TRAM 3, 9, 14, 24
ACCESS open

Václav Havel and Stanislav Bechyně (engineering)

Hradčany to Nové Město

Vodičkova Building 1907–10, Štěpánská Building 1913–21

U Nováků Palace

U Nováků Palace, originally a department store, is a Secession building dripping with a wealth of decorative elements both inside and out. The variety of design to the façade, in colour, texture, materials and form, is astonishing. Allow time just to observe the whole Vodičkova elevation. This is a narrow street, busy with passing trams and cars, and the buildings on either side appear surprisingly tall, making it difficult to absorb the architectural richness. The façade mosaic, a usual Prague Secessionist feature, is particularly attractive and is based on a design by Jan Preisler (1872–1918), a Czech painter, showing an allegory of Business and Industry. In the basement is a variety theatre which was used by Osvobozené divadlo (Liberated Theatre), showing famous Voskovec and Werich shows in the 1930s.

Also take a look at two interesting Secession buildings, Praha Insurance Company and Topič House, at Národní 7 and 9 / 1011, 1010, Praha 1 Staré Město, also by Osvald Polívka (1907–08). Topič is rather spoiled by the brutal shop conversion which eliminated its more subtle original Secession base.

ADDRESS Vodičkova 30 / 699, Praha 1 Nové Město
METRO Můstek – Lines A and B
TRAM 3, 9, 14, 24
ACCESS open

Osvald Polívka 1902–1903

Hradčany to Nové Město

Osvald Polívka 1902–1903

Retail and Apartment Building, Palackého

Zelenka's favourite building material was the glass block, perhaps used under the influence of Le Corbusier's Porte Molitor apartments (1933) or Pierre Chareau's Maison de Verre (1927–32). Large areas of glass blocks certainly add another dimension to the interior by refining the light, making inner spaces airy, pleasant and somewhat mysterious. With the south-west-facing façade Zelenka had the perfect opportunity to conjure up this atmosphere.

Zelenka was also a theatre set, costume and graphic designer creating interesting proposals for plays staged at Osvobozené divadlo. His posters for the Aero company, manufacturing innovative front-wheel drive, two-stroke engine sports cars, were especially appealing.

At Národní 30 / 59, Praha 1 Nové Město, the present Špála Gallery used to be Vilímek Publishers for whom Zelenka designed, in 1938, a chromed steel shopfront with neon sign and entrance doors with cut-out perforations. It remains the most stunning 1930s' doorway in Prague.

ADDRESS Palackého 9 / 718, Praha 1 Nové Město
METRO Můstek – Lines A and B
TRAM 3, 9, 14, 24
ACCESS ground floor open

František Zelenka 1937

František Zelenka 1937

Diamant House and Arch

A retail and apartment building, situated on the corner of Spálená and Lazarská, with Cubist overtones like the treatment of the columns by the entrance to the apartments and the sculptural decoration at roof level. It is similar in appearance and detail to the Moravian Bank on Wenceslas Square. Do not miss the well-designed house signs made from metal rods attached to the façade facing Lazarská.

Another nice touch, with its combination of styles, is the Cubist arch with metalwork infills framing the Baroque statue of St John Nepomuk by Jan Michal Brokoff (1717) next to the Church of Holy Trinity by Ottavio Broggio (1712–13).

ADDRESS Spálená 4 / 82, Praha 1 Nové Město
METRO Národní třída – Line B
TRAM 6, 9, 18, 22
ACCESS ground floor open

Emil Králíček and Matěj Blecha 1912–13

Emil Králíček and Matěj Blecha 1912–13

Olympic Building

The initial design for this building graces the pages of all the books on Czech 20th century architecture. This was the first true modern office building proposal for Prague. Now, hemmed in between its neighbours, its special quality is not as plainly visible as when it was finished in 1926.

The design clearly illustrates the conception of urban life envisaged by the avant-garde movement Devětsil. The lower levels were occupied by shops, cafés and restaurants. Above, in the upper levels, were offices and apartments. The roof terrace and balconies were edged with nautically inspired balustrades, stripped window awnings shaded the openings and large advertisements in bold letters were painted on the exposed party wall. These motifs were tools of Devětsil which emphasised the power of graphic design for signs and slogans and its effect on the life of the city inhabitants.

Recent insensitive refurbishment has sadly destroyed the contemporary interiors.

ADDRESS Spálená 16 / 75, Praha 1
Nové Město
METRO Národní třída – Line B
TRAM 6, 9, 18, 22
ACCESS none

Jaromír Krejcar 1923–26

Hradčany to Nové Město

Jaromír Krejcar 1923–26

Czechoslovak Decorative Arts Federation Building

Starý and Zelenka's building contains an art gallery in the basement, shops at ground- and first-floor levels, along a walk-through arcade, and offices on the upper floors placed within a tight L-shaped site fronting on to Národní třída and a little street called Charvátova. The façade to Národní has the top floor reduced visually to decrease its bulk and to conform to the planning regulations and the columns are set back from the slab edges. It is almost fully glazed, divided by a grid of narrow floor bands and thin vertical mullions giving it a similar transparent treatment to Kysela's Lindt and Baťa buildings.

The court of the arcade, placed at the junction of the two wings, has rounded internal corners and a glazed roof. The central part of the roof is retractable allowing more light to penetrate inside and revealing a view of the rear elevation. The contemporary semicircular wall light fittings complement the overall concept. The Charvátova façade was designed by František Zelenka.

Another early Functionalist building is the Chicago at Národní 32 / 58 with an entrance in Charvátova, by Josef Havlíček and Jaroslav Polívka (1927–28).

ADDRESS Národní 36 / 38, Praha 1 Nové Město
METRO Národní třída – Line B
TRAM 6, 9, 18, 22
ACCESS shops, gallery and arcade open

Hradčany to Nové Město

Oldřich Starý and František Zelenka 1934–38

Oldřich Starý and František Zelenka 1934–38

Máj Department Store, now K-Mart

A bold building constructed by Swedish firm NCC International AB of Solna, but not suited to the sensitive location of Na Perštýně junction. The main problem is the response of the building to the corner of Národní and Spálená. The blank, diagonally striped concrete panel side is attractive in itself but is unkind to pedestrians and the buildings opposite with its brutal expression and vast expanse. The smooth shiny façade facing Národní, although it recedes at the top, is too long and uninterrupted, letting the containment of the street atmosphere slip out along its white and glass surface.

The rear, fully glazed elevation opening towards the Národní třída metro station is more successful with the bank of escalators behind allowing shoppers to observe city life while moving between the store's floors. Similarly from outside, especially in the evening, this side of the building is animated with movement and light.

ADDRESS Národní 26 / 63, Praha 1 Nové Město
METRO Národní třída – Line B
TRAM 6, 9, 18, 22
ACCESS open

SIAL: Miroslav Masák, John Eisler and Martin Rajniš 1970–75

SIAL: Miroslav Masák, John Eisler and Martin Rajniš 1970–75

Nová Scéna National Theatre

The National Theatre was originally built between 1868 and 1881 to the design of Josef Zítek. Money for the building was collected throughout the nation and therefore the theatre can truly be called national. After a fire in 1881 the theatre was rebuilt and extended by Josef Schulz. The interior was lavishly decorated by leading Czech artists of the period.

Several competitions were held before the Second World War, and since 1958, for additional spaces required by the theatre. Between 1977 and 1981 Pavel Kupka, from the State Institute for Reconstruction, designed and built the south administration and operations building and the east café and restaurant wing. In 1980 the Prague Institute for Construction, led by Karel Prager, was commissioned to complete the extension.

The accommodation in the new north wing consisted of an entrance foyer and an open, square-shaped auditorium. The Nová Scéna (New Stage) was clad with 4306 specially blown glass sound-insulation blocks of 80 x 60 x 40 cm, each weighing 40 kg and made at the Kavalier works, Sázava. There were several design solutions before the final rather severe and solid but simple option was chosen. One suspects that the architect's choice of this monumental cladding material, set alight by the evening sun, was fuelled by the desire to display the skills of the Bohemian glassmakers.

ADDRESS Národní 4 / 1393, Praha 1 Nové Město
METRO Národní třída – Line B
TRAM 6, 9, 18, 21, 22,
ACCESS open during performances

Karel Prager 1980–83

Hradčany to Nové Město

Hlahol House

A house designed and built for the Hlahol men's choir which was established in 1861. The composition is strongly influenced by the Viennese Secession. The central flat section of the building is framed by two richer end elements with convex balconies, concave windows and sculptural reliefs. The main entrance to the hall has a tiled phoenix over the door arch. The timber door is softly carved with flower motifs. The contemporary ironmongery fittings and signs complete the picture. The decorative reliefs are by Josef Pekárek and the mosaic on the main gable, representing music and other ornamentation, is by Karel Mottl.

Three plaques commemorate famous people from the musical world who were connected with the Hlahol Choral Society – Karel Bendl, Bedřich Smetana and Karel Knittl. Smetana, best known for his comic opera Prodaná nevěsta (The Bartered Bride, 1865) and symphonic cycle Má vlast (My Country, 1875–80), was a chorus master of the Hlahol for several years from 1862.

ADDRESS Masarykovo nábřeží 16 / 248,
PRAHA 1 Nové Město
METRO Karlovo náměstí – Line B
TRAM 17
ACCESS none

Josef Fanta, Čeněk Gregor and František Schlaffer 1903–06

Josef Fanta, Čeněk Gregor and František Schlaffer 1903–06

Mánes Building

The Šítkovský water mill existed here in the 12th century and was extended in 1495 to contain the town water works and tank tower. After several reconstructions only the old tower, with a Baroque onion dome roof, remained. The tower supplied water to town fountains. In 1928 the site was cleared and a white Functionalist building housing a restaurant, club room and gallery for the artistic group Mánes, which was founded in 1887, was erected there. Novotný rather romantically followed the notion of the mill buildings bridging the river channel from the Masaryk Embankment to Slovanský Island. The gallery is open to the busy quay side while the restaurant is turned towards the river and the green island.

Mánes is a favourite modern building of President Václav Havel who has fond memories of being watched, while living in his apartment on the Rašín Embankment, by the Czech Secret Service, hidden at the top of the ancient water tower, during the dark days of Communism.

ADDRESS Masarykovo nábřeží 1 / 250, Praha 1 Nové Město
METRO Karlovo náměstí – Line B
TRAM 3, 17
ACCESS open

Otakar Novotný 1927–30 (first studies 1923–25)

Otakar Novotný 1927–30 (first studies 1923–25)

Vinohrady to Vyšehrad

Office Centre Vinohrady 128
Agricultural Institute 130
Gymnasium 132
Laichter House 134
Prague Main Railway Station (Hlavní nádraží) 136
Commercial Building, Rašínovo nábřeží 138
Church Tower, Na Slovanech (Emauzy) 140
Social Security and Health Ministries 142
Hlava Pathology Institute 144
Villa Kovařovič 146
Apartment Building, Neklanova 148
Hodek Apartment Building 150
Hodek, Bayer and Belada House 154

Office Centre Vinohrady

This fine building was one of the first speculative office developments built in Prague since the Velvet Revolution and illustrates the difficulty of designing for unknown occupiers and their specific requirements. The architects have skilfully directed their artistic efforts to cope with the external envelope and the entrance foyer which creates a strong identity for the building. In the Loos tradition, a simple block form with a rounded corner faced in rich natural materials of polished grey-green granite contrasts with the clear varnished timber of the horizontal windows to proclaim the building's dignified presence.

The adjacent block in Balbínova and Vinohradská is an interesting Functionalist building occupied by the Czech Broadcasting Company (Bohumil Sláma, 1927–30) which might have inspired the proportions of the Office Centre.

See also another ADNS offices project at Anglická 20, Praha 2 Vinohrady, from 1994–95.

Nearby at Francouzská 4 / 75, Praha 2 Vinohrady, is Jaromír Krejcar's building for the Society of Self-Employed Clerical Workers (1927–31) and at Francouzská 14 / 175 is Josef Mach's interesting retail and apartment building from 1938–39.

ADDRESS Římská 15 / 499, Praha 2 Vinohrady
METRO Náměstí Míru – Line A
TRAM 4, 11, 16, 22
ACCESS none

ADNS: V. Alda, P. Dvořák, M. Němec, J. Stempel 1993–94

Vinohrady to Vyšehrad

ADNS: V. Alda, P. Dvořák, M. Němec, J. Stempel 1993–94

Agricultural Institute

Remarkably straight-forward architecture for the early 1920s. This building's concept, however, is still influenced by the Cubist style in the stacking of the forms and the sharp projecting corners, edges and angles. The arrangement of the short elevation facing towards the length of Slezká is especially attractive. The large central bay, with its expressed structural frame, is punctuated with window openings and bordered by wings, which are further supported by tall staircase towers. The bright red of the facing brickwork advertises the Institute from a distance, particularly when the rays of the morning sun lift the surface sheen.

Vinohrady to Vyšehrad

ADDRESS Slezká 7 / 100, Praha 2 Vinohrady
METRO Náměstí Míru – Line A
TRAM 11, 16
ACCESS none

Josef Gočár 1924–26

Josef Gočár 1924–26

Gymnasium

Long black columns marching along the pavement contrast with the bulk of this white-tiled structure. They appear like purposeful massive legs clothed in smart dark trousers. The form of the sloping soffit, diagonally cutting the tops of columns, reflects the floor of the auditorium within. The window openings regularly punched into the long elevation and the end staircase enclosure, with its diagonal windows and roof sloping the opposite way, all add to this impressive and well-engineered Functionalist building.

The park setting of Riegerovy sady (Rieger Orchards), founded in 1902 and named after a Czech politician, mellows the hard-edged architecture. Ceramic tiles were a popular cladding material in the late 1920s and 1930s in Czechoslovakia, a trademark of the period, and proved to be a long-lasting and maintenance-free external finish.

Vinohrady to Vyšehrad

ADDRESS Polská 1 / 2400, Praha 2 Vinohrady
METRO Jiřího z Poděbrad – Line A
TRAM 11
ACCESS none

František Marek, Zbyněk Jirsák and Václav Vejrych 1938–46

František Marek, Zbyněk Jirsák and Václav Vejrych 1938–46

Laichter House

A house combining a small publishing business with private accommodation for the owner, Jan Laichter, similar in style and simplicity to Jan Kotěra's other work from the same period – Villa Kotěra at Hradešínská and Urbánek House at Jungmannova. This building belongs to the rational Modernism period, an architectural attitude developed as a reaction to the Secession under the influence of Berlage and Wright. The function of the inner spaces is clearly and formally expressed on the outside and, typically, exposed brickwork is used as the external finish. Decoration is kept to a minimum, using the bricks to create simple geometric patterns. Bands of render supply a broader divisional framework for the whole composition.

Next door, at Chopinova 6 / 1556, is an interesting apartment house with late Secessionist decorations by Bohumil Waigant from 1910.

Vinohrady to Vyšehrad

ADDRESS Chopinova 4 / 1543, Praha 2 Vinohrady
METRO Jiřího z Poděbrad – Line a
TRAM 11
ACCESS none

Jan Kotěra 1908–09

Vinohrady to Vyšehrad

Jan Kotěra 1908–09

Prague Main Railway Station (Hlavní nádraží)

Also called President Wilson Station, and, before the First World War, named Emperor Franz-Josef Station, this late Secession creation was loosely based on the Gare du Nord in Paris. The half-cylindrical vaulted central hall is expressed on the outside of the main elevation by a large glazed arch which signifies a gateway to the city. Rich sculptural decorations and motifs from incompatible styles are brought together in a well-considered synthesis. Glass globes representing the Earth sit on top of the two square towers bordering the glazed arch. Further buildings either side of the entrance hall accommodate the railway administration. A park, Riegerovy sady, beyond forms a soft green backdrop. Sculptures are by Ladislav Šaloun, Stanislav Sucharda and Čeněk Vosmík.

These days, sadly, the station is cut off from pedestrians by the preposterous six-lane *magistrála*. Now, the only way to approach the building is to enter the large dingy hall built under the dual carriageway between 1971 and 1979 (Josef Bočan, Josef Danda, Alena Šrámková, Jan Šrámek) and miss the impact of coming to the station as Fanta envisaged: under the glass canopy with a porter wheeling a pile of suitcases behind you while the whistle of the Berlin–Vienna express summoning the late travellers to the platform echoed through the station concourse.

ADDRESS Wilsonova 8 / 300, Praha 2 Vinohrady
METRO Hlavní nádraží – Line C
ACCESS open

Josef Fanta 1901–09

Josef Fanta 1901–09

Commercial Building, Rašínovo nábřeží

This is a highly controversial 5000-square-metre scheme designed for a Dutch developer, Nationale Nederlanden. It is situated on one of the few empty sites in Prague, courtesy of Anglo-American bombing at the end of the Second World War, and adjacent to the building erected by the President's grandfather, Vácslav Havel. Lengthy correspondence and discussions in professional circles and publications have developed about the building's suitability within Prague's urban environment.

The main concerns have been whether the Gehry creation would be appropriate to end the embankment block towards Jirásek Square, its response to the neighbouring architecture of the turn of the century apartment buildings and its face towards the river.

Gehry's building has been nicknamed 'Ginger Rogers and Fred Astaire' because of the two corner cylinder elements, one of double-layered flared glass and one solid, supporting a wave-patterned façade. It is an odd and idiosyncratic building which has no roots or origins in central European culture. Rather than contributing to Prague's townscape it exposes itself as a flamboyant advertisement for its creators.

ADDRESS Rašínovo nábřeží 80, Praha 2 Nové Město
METRO Karlovo náměstí – Line B
TRAM 3, 4, 7, 16, 17
ACCESS ground floor and roof top restaurant open

Frank O. Gehry & Associates with Vlado Milunič 1993–95

Frank O. Gehry & Associates with Vlado Milunič 1993–95

Church Tower, Na Slovanech (Emauzy)

The Gothic Church of the Virgin Mary and Saints Jeronym, Cyril and Metoděj is attached to the Benedictine monastery, Na Slovanech or Emauzy, which was founded in 1347 by King Charles IV. The church was consecrated in 1372. In the 17th century the original Gothic building was altered and transformed into the Baroque style with two church towers on the west façade. The church was badly damaged by the Anglo-American air raid on 14 February 1945. Renovation started immediately but the choice of tower replacement was left to be resolved by competition.

After two series of submissions Černý's modern and daring solution overtook the more traditional proposals. The idea of the reinforced concrete shell in the form of two crossing wings evoked the original single Gothic gable as well as the twin Baroque version in a single arrangement and another tower has been added to the Prague panorama. However, the new tower sits rather uncomfortably on the stubby ancient wall and a more extended and solid base would have improved the composition.

Vinohrady to Vyšehrad

ADDRESS Vyšehradská 49 / 320, Praha 2 Nové Město
METRO Karlovo náměstí – Line B
TRAM 18, 24
ACCESS open during services

František M. Černý and Vladimír Kamberský 1965–1968

Vinohrady to Vyšehrad

František M. Černý and Vladimír Kamberský 1965–1968

Social Security and Health Ministries

A dramatic and allegorical monument to František Palacký, a prominent Czech historian and patriot, by Stanislav Sucharda, with architectural setting by Alois Dryák (1898–1907), contrasts sharply with the soft and subtle modelling of render and travertine finishes of the ministry buildings designed as part of the grand masterplan for the urban plaza.

In 1907 Prague's planning department arranged a competition for the urban treatment of the large square. The resulting studies, however, obscured the view of Emauzy Monastery. Second-stage submissions by Vlastislav Hofman (1912) and Bohumil Hypšman (1913) showed improved concepts. Nothing was done until Hypšman pushed through his pre-war design in 1923. His design separated the two ministry buildings, allowing views on to the monastery, and framed and enclosed the square with pergolas, terraces and balustrades on several levels. The square is calm and restful but, without the attraction of shops and restaurants, lacks the necessary signs of life of a modern city.

Vinohrady to Vyšehrad

ADDRESS Palackého náměstí 4 / 375, Na poříčském právu 1 / 376, Praha 2 Nové Město
METRO Karlovo náměstí – Line B
TRAM 18, 24
ACCESS none to the buildings

Bohumil Hypšman 1923–31

Bohumil Hypšman 1923–31

Hlava Pathology Institute

The Institute, named after Jaroslav Hlava (1855–1924), a founder of Czech modern pathology, contains departments for pathology, judicial medicine, bacteriology and autopsy. Due to the lighting requirements of the autopsy rooms the building was planned in the form of a J. The north wing, the short curved section, with fully glazed semicircular bays allowed maximum light penetration without direct sunlight, making these spaces ideal for post-mortem medical examination. Originally, the roofs of the bay windows were also glazed.

The long east elevation contains a lecture hall which is projected out and expressed on the façade by tall vertically stepped windows. A remarkably early rational building design perfectly encloses the functional requirements of pathology.

ADDRESS Studničkova 2–4 / 2039 II, Praha 2 Nové Město
METRO I.P. Pavlova – Line C
TRAM 18, 24
ACCESS none

Alois Špalek 1913–21

Vinohrady to Vyšehrad

Alois Špalek 1913–21

Villa Kovařovič

There is an extraordinary assembly of Cubist-style buildings arranged around a small area under the Vyšehrad rock. The Villa Kovařovič shares its small island site with two other notable buildings. On the right is the Modernist Villa Sequens by Otakar Novotný (1912–13), on the left a Neo-classical villa by Emil Králíček (1912–13) with Cubist interior details.

Josef Chochol always tried to keep pace with the latest fashion which, at that time, was the Cubist style of architecture derived from the paintings of Picasso and Braque. He applied the style beyond the building to include the garden layout and the surrounding walls using shaped flower beds, levels, steps, planting, rendered brick walls and metalwork to echo the façades of the villa. The three-dimensional quality of the villa was reinforced by the design of the side façades of which the upper parts are visible from the street. The play of light and shadow on the pyramidal and crystal forms constantly changes the massing of the building and animates it.

Complex fragmentation was applied by Cubist architects to express their style, but the play of form could go no further than the manipulation of façades, with distorted windows, metalwork screens, floor and wall decorations, ceiling patterning and sharp-angled ironmongery design. The floor plans generally remained quite conventional to make the buildings reasonably habitable. However, stunning pieces of furniture and decorative arts were produced to complement the Cubist exteriors.

ADDRESS Libušina 3 / 49, Praha 2 Vyšehrad
METRO Vyšehrad – Line C
TRAM 3, 7, 17
BUS 148
ACCESS none

Josef Chochol 1912–13

Josef Chochol 1912–13

Apartment Building, Neklanova

This apartment building has a plain subtle façade except for the heavy oversailing cornice with Cubist folded-fabric motifs. Its impact is due to the contrast between the handling of the façade and the cornice, and it is a very mild version of a Hodek building further along the same street. It is possible that the architect Josef Chochol was also involved here and advised on the design of this house for Antonín Belada, who was a builder.

ADDRESS Neklanova 2 / 56, Praha 2 Vyšehrad
METRO Vyšehrad – Line C
TRAM 7, 18, 24
BUS 148
ACCESS none

Antonín Belada 1913

Antonín Belada 1913

Vinohrady to Vyšehrad

Hodek Apartment Building

At the beginning of this century, at the height of the Secession period, architects, painters and sculptors worked together to create richly decorated buildings with paintings, mosaics and sculptures in a common style. It was followed, under the influence of Dutch and American architecture, by a more sober, Modernist approach to architecture, adopted in Bohemia by Jan Kotěra and Otakar Novotný.

Some Czech architects (Pavel Janák, Josef Gočár, Vlastislav Hofman, and Josef Chochol) rebelled against this attitude, which they thought too simplistic, and which cut them off from working with other artists. They therefore welcomed with enthusiasm the Cubist style of painting as another common inspiration which could bring all the arts together again, and formed their own group, Skupina výtvarných umělců, to support their new attitude to design.

Chochol's motto 'new equals better' involved him with Cubism with maximum impulse and that is clearly manifested in the Hodek Building. This is one of the most extraordinary Cubist creations, perfectly exploiting the street-corner position and giving focus to the whole composition.

At the junction of the two building faces a smooth octagonal upright supports a magnificent, umbrella-like cornice which spreads from the corner along the length of both elevations and is reinforced by the distorted windows and crystal solids of the façades. In this setting, Chochol's elevations can be viewed at the same time, in the same way that Cubist painters showed their subjects from all sides on a two-dimensional canvas to illustrate their all-encompassing approach. Cubist ideas spread inside the entrance hall as shaped doors and modelled brass kick plates, 'folded' door handles, and floor and wall details.

The apartments, apart from where the front elevation affects the inte-

Josef Chochol 1913–14

rior, are plain and conventional. In fact, the rear courtyard elevation is square and rigid, almost Purist, giving the building two sides. Chochol has thrown a Cubist coat over a modest humble body. The design of this building should be an inspiration for those eager to dabble in Deconstructivism.

ADDRESS Neklanova 30 / 98, Praha 2 Vyšehrad
METRO Vyšehrad – Line C
TRAM 7, 18, 24
BUS 148
ACCESS none

Josef Chochol 1913–14

Josef Chochol 1913–14

Hodek, Bayer and Belada House

A Cubist 'triple' house built for František Hodek, Jan and Josef Bayer and Antonín Belada, its design based on the disposition of a Baroque palace.

The middle house, facing the river, has a large decorative gable and sculptures which do not conform to the Cubist style. The end houses have their main elevations and entrances turned to each side. The heavy, rendered brick façade is carried on into the Mansard roof by the masonry surrounding the dormer windows. The play of forms is underlined by the large side elevation bay windows and delicate detailing of the frames.

Internally, the Cubist motifs are seen in the tiling of the floors and the decorative ceilings.'

ADDRESS Rašínovo nábřeží 6–10 / 42, 47, 71, Praha 2 Vyšehrad
METRO Vyšehrad – Line C
TRAM 3, 7, 17
BUS 148
ACCESS none

Josef Chochol 1912–13

Josef Chochol 1912–13

Žižkov and Vinohrady

General Pensions Institute 158
National Monument 160
Church of the Sacred Heart 162
Franz Kafka's Tombstone 166

General Pensions Institute

This is a classic group of buildings of Functionalist architecture, one of the first air-conditioned buildings in Europe, often published since completion. The complex of buildings consists of different height wings arranged at right angles to one another and accommodating offices, shops and apartments.

The beige rectangular ceramic tiles on the façades give the buildings a tidy and precise quality. The pronounced horizontality provided by the timber windows contrasts with the vertical glazed band of the end elevations. The solid sections between the windows are covered with mosaic tiles. Architectural elements at ground level are faced in pale blue tiles giving the building a variety of textures and hues despite its uniformity. The tubular balustrade at roof level is also designed to sprinkle water on to the tiled elevations for cleaning.

To obtain the desired tile finish was quite a battle. The client was insistent that he could only afford an external render. However, the close proximity of the Main Railway Station, in the age of steam engines, worried the architects. They prepared a sample panel of the render, covered one half, then left it to weather for a few weeks. After another stormy site meeting, when discussion turned again to the external finish, the client was persuaded to view the sample. After the architects revealed the protected white sample against the already dark grey exposed side, the client immediately agreed to the use of Rako ceramic tiles.

ADDRESS Náměstí W. Churchilla 2 / 1800, 1839, 1840, Praha 3 Žižkov
METRO Hlavní nádraží – Line c
TRAM 5, 9, 26
ACCESS none

Žižkov and Vinohrady

Josef Havlíček and Karel Honzík 1929–33

Josef Havlíček and Karel Honzík 1929–33

National Monument

Here Jan Žižka (1360–1424), a famous Czech warrior, won a battle, supported by Praguers, against the anti-Hussite crusader troops of Emperor Sigismund on 14 July 1420. It was a decisive battle against Sigismund's onslaught and lead to his defeat. Because of this historical association the National Monument was placed on this hill.

A competition was held in 1913 and received some interesting Cubist entries but, in the end, the outcome was unresolved. Sculptor František Bílek had proposed, for example, a 10-metre-high statue of Žižka which was to have been approached by an avenue formed from 20 giant rocks.

After the First World War, Jan Zázvorka was chosen to execute the project. The result is an austere granite-clad building containing a tomb for the Unknown Soldier. In the upper part of the Monument is the main hall with anteroom and viewing galleries and below is the mausoleum in which the embalmed body of the first Czechoslovak Communist President, Klement Gottwald, was placed, along with the remains of his political comrades. The interior is faced in marble and decorated with reliefs and mosaics by leading Czech artists Max Švabinský, Karel Pokorný, Jakub Obrovský, and others.

The equestrian statue of Žižka by Bohumil Kafka (1878–1942), supposedly the largest such bronze sculpture in the world, weighing 16.5 tonnes, was completed between 1931 and 1941 and placed here in 1950.

ADDRESS Vítkov 1900, Praha 3 Žižkov
METRO Florenc – Line C
TRAM 5, 9, 26
BUS 133, 168, 207
ACCESS intermitent

Žižkov and Vinohrady

Jan Zázvorka 1926–32

Žižkov and Vinohrady

Jan Zázvorka 1926–32

Church of the Sacred Heart

This extraordinary building, perhaps Plečnik's best, was designed over a number of years. Plečnik proposed several options, starting in 1922, progressing from an idea based on a temple similar to the Parthenon in Athens but with an additional, separate, tall bell tower placed by one corner. To reduce costs, the next proposal showed a single-nave church, with a more massive tower, whose façade was treated with his popular design tools, semicircular arches and motifs. However, none of these designs was as unusual or original as the final version from 1927 on which work began on site two years later.

The church is enclosed in a dark brown brick cloak with an 'upturned collar'-like cornice which is encrusted with a geometric decoration of grey granite stones, and out of which another building of a different style rises. The outward-leaning cornice is a similar detail to Cubist buildings by Josef Chochol at Vyšehrad. The door portals mimic the form of the rest of the building, appearing like the backs of priests' robes, unifying the whole composition. The unusual massive tower, located on a centre line created by Laubkova Street, is more than 42 metres high. Large, clear glass-faced dials of the clock, 7.6 metres in diameter, lighten the mass of the tower. The clock and the bells are accessed by a daring, thin reinforced-concrete ramp.

The church interior, organised as one nave, has red brick walls decorated with gilded crosses and modulated by regular pilasters. Under the polished coffered timber ceiling clerestory windows sit on the white walkway, supplying daylight into the nave. The nave floor is laid in terrazzo with circular grey and red patterns and square marble blocks. The six statues of Czech patron saints and the central sculpture representing the Sacred Heart, placed on the wall above the main altar, were designed by Plečnik and carved by the sculptor Damian Pešan. The

Jože Plečnik 1922–33

Jože Plečnik 1922–33

tunnel-like crypt faced in scabbled brickwork has light slots terminating at the nave floor. The construction of the church was supervised by Otto Rothmayer, who also looked after Plečnik's projects at Prague Castle.

One has to walk around the building several times to appreciate its complex mood, the ever-changing form and pattern of the façade which keeps altering, depending on the viewpoint and time of the day.

Žižkov and Vinohrady

ADDRESS Náměstí Jiřího z Poděbrad, Praha 3 Vinohrady
METRO Jiřího z Poděbrad – Line A
TRAM 11
ACCESS open during services

Jože Plečnik 1922–33

Jože Plečnik 1922–33

Franz Kafka's Tombstone

To come here is to pay homage to one of the great men of Prague and his literary estate. The crystal form of the writer's tombstone represents not only Franz Kafka (1883–1924) but also another Prague phenomenon, Cubist architecture, showing an architectural creativity very rarely practised nowadays.

In 1911 the architect Pavel Janák identified two form-making forces in nature: the horizontal level of water and the vertical direction of weight. Other more complicated forms were created by a third diagonal force, a power resident within matter. The best example of this power is in crystallisation. The force concentrated within the crystals is so strong that it overcomes weight. If vertical and horizontal planes are the forms of calmness and balance of matter, diagonally shaped forms are created by more dramatic action and the complicated union of forces. By inclusion of the third, diagonal plane one can implant soul into matter and convey dramatic action.

There was no better way to symbolise Kafka's complex personality which gave the world his far-reaching literary achievement than by using a crystal form and all the energy and mystery it encapsulated.

I was surprised to discover that my great grandfather, who also died in 1924, lies buried head to head with the creator of Josef K. Prague is, after all, a small city.

ADDRESS Židovské hřbitovy, Nad vodovodem 1 / 712, plot no. 21 14 33, Praha 3 Žižkov
METRO Želivského – Line A
TRAM 11, 16, 19, 26
ACCESS Sunday to Thursday, September to March, 8.00–15.00, April to August, 8.00–16.00; men are asked to cover their heads

Leopold Ehrmann 1924

Leopold Ehrmann 1924

Podolí to Hodkovičky

Water Filtration Works 170
Swimming Pool Stadium 172
Water Tower 174
Villa Langer 176
Villa Dvořák 178
Villa Frič 180

Water Filtration Works

Antonín Engel was one of the few Prague protagonists of classical architecture and this building illustrates clearly the tensions between the modern and the conservative. It is a curious and massive block, a mixture of traditionalism with modern touches, such as the use of glass blocks which glow at night and reflect the water of the river and passing street life during the day. The continuous, almost too frequent, rhythm of the classical perimeter columns gives order and animation to the façades. It repeats at the upper levels with shallower piers and circular window openings. With sculptures added to the cornices, the building appears like a cathedral enclosing a sacred water well.

Podolí to Hodkovičky

ADDRESS Podolská 17 / 15, Praha 4 Podolí
TRAM 3, 17
ACCESS none

Antonín Engel 1923–28

Antonín Engel 1923–28

Swimming Pool Stadium

The stadium is built on the site of an old quarry. An elegantly shaped roof covers a pool (20 x 50 metres) with seating for 700 visitors and also provides an auditorium for 4500 spectators above two open swimming pool areas. The sculptural arrangement of diving boards and other decorative artwork adds interest to the large tiled podium between the pools and other sports facilities. This is a popular place for swimming, relaxing and watching the sun go down.

Podolí to Hodkovičky

ADDRESS Podolská 74 / 43, Praha 4 Podolí
TRAM 3, 17
ACCESS Monday to Friday 6.00–22.00, Saturday and Sunday 8.00–22.00

Richard F. Podzemný and Gustav Kuchař 1958–65

Richard F. Podzemný and Gustav Kuchař 1958–65

Water Tower

An early example of evocative industrial architecture of remarkable design quality. Some elements are handled with the delicacy of a product designer. The brickwork is skilfully executed with strong patterning. The entrance door is framed with a rounded arch supported by stub columns and the main brick piers rising up to the water tank are held in position by 'slotted grooves' on the underside of the container. The whole structure is topped with a handsome helmet-shaped roof.

Podolí to Hodkovičky

ADDRESS Hanusova 5 / 1121, Praha 4 Michle
METRO Budějovická – Line C
BUS 118, 124, 134, 157, 178, 190, 192, 193
ACCESS none

Jan Kotěra 1906–07

Podolí to Hodkovičky

Jan Kotěra 1906–07

Villa Langer

This simple villa was built for František Langer (1888–1965), a dramatist, soldier and doctor. The architect, Karel Honzík, was also an author and in his theoretical work explained his attitude to designing small domestic buildings.

'Just as the war brought about tremendous progress in science and industry, so the villa has become a laboratory of new construction techniques and materials and an opportunity for training in and improving the crafts. The problems of layout and functionality, which the villa has highlighted, have become a focal point of architectural work, to be applied to the design of large structures and to become the basis of a new architectural methodology. Most modern villas were built for members of the intellectual classes, who were aware of the need to help the architect to seek forms of construction that would best express the basic requirements of life inside the house.'

ADDRESS Nad cementárnou 23 / 331, Praha 4 Podolí
METRO Pražského povstání – Line C
TRAM 3, 17
ACCESS none

Karel Honzík 1929–30

Karel Honzík 1929–30

Villa Dvořák

Like a precious stone among a sea of pebbles, this cubed whitewashed villa stands out from the surrounding development of pretentious, over-designed houses. The concept of this small family house continues the tradition of Miesian architecture with carefully placed openings in the white solid cubic form and a clear arrangement of spaces. The living room, kitchen, bathroom and two small bedrooms are at the top. The entrance floor is reached by a short flight of steel stairs from the garden, with a studio, guest room and utility room at lower level. The villa was self-built by the owner, a painter, to drawings supplied by Jan Kaplický.

Another project in Prague by Kaplický (apart from the Memorial to the Victims of Communism; see page 36) is a concave memorial plaque to Franz Kafka (1966) placed on the house of Kafka's birth on the corner of Maiselova and Staroměstské náměstí, Praha 1 Staré Město.

see page 36

Podolí to Hodkovičky

ADDRESS Na Dobešce 1 / 1239, Praha 4 Bráník
TRAM 3, 17
BUS 124, 178
ACCESS none

Jan Kaplický 1967

Jan Kaplický 1967

Villa Frič

Accessible only by a steep, narrow, overgrown driveway, this villa appears to sail through the surrounding gardens like a streamlined boat. The architect, Ladislav Žák, continually took inspiration from the form of ocean liners and aeroplanes. The top floor includes interconnected living, dining and study spaces. An external terrace with a winter garden opens onto the dining area and a small kitchen. The bedrooms are located on the ground floor with a terrace turned towards the garden. Although in need of renovation, original furniture and fittings designed by Žák are still there as provided almost 60 years ago.

Martin Frič (1902–68) was a film director and actor who, in the 1930s, became one of the most sought after personalities in the Czech film industry. His bust can be seen by the entrance to Max Urban's Barrandov Film Studios.

Podolí to Hodkovičky

ADDRESS Na lysinách 15 / 208, Praha 4 Hodkovičky
BUS 121
ACCESS none

Ladislav Žák 1934–35

Podolí to Hodkovičky

Ladislav Žák 1934–35

Smíchov to Hlubočepy

Speech Therapy Clinic 184
Villa Winternitz 186
Villa Jíše 188
Water Pressure Equalisation Tower 190
Barrandov Film Studios 192
Villa, Barrandovská 194
Barrandov Restaurant 196
Swimming Pool, Barrandov 198

Speech Therapy Clinic

The conversion and extension of a family villa designed by Josef Falout (1930–31) transformed this small building into an interesting modern addition to Prague's public buildings. The villa was extended on the right side and a Miesian grid of white trellis was thrown over to unify the horizontal and vertical planes. The attractive glazed barrel vault covering the entrance courtyard indicates a route through the building, which passes across an entrance hall and a well-equipped play room, to the garden. It is extended by an elevated metal grille walkway ending with a fabulous view over the city.

In the garden a wind-powered roundabout set into a cobblestoned hollow adds motion and colour to the cool and simple setting.

ADDRESS U Mrázovky 15 / 1970,
Praha 5 Smíchov
METRO Anděl – Line B
TRAM 4, 7, 9
BUS 137
ACCESS none

Smíchov to Hlubočepy

D.A. Studio: Martin Rajniš and collective 1984–87

Smíchov to Hlubočepy

D.A. Studio: Martin Rajniš and collective 1984–87

Villa Winternitz

This is a relatively unknown Loos villa in Prague. It seems to be the opposite of the Villa Müller in Střešovice. Built later, it certainly displays more external expression and modelling, perhaps to the detriment of the handling of the interior normally expected from Loos. The villa has been used as a kindergarten for some time and the interior has been adjusted to cope with children's needs and activities – window safety grilles testify to the change of use.

Strangely, the villa seems to ignore the attractive view over Prague to the rear and its primary façade and living spaces are turned towards the street, the warmer south side. The main symmetrical volumes of the building interlock, dovetailing perfectly into each other like pieces of a three-dimensional jigsaw. The grid of the structure extended over the south roof terrace completes the massing of the house, keeping it in the correct proportions and adding interest to the roofscape.

The living room, one and a half storeys high, runs the full width of the villa and has three large windows into the garden. Half a level up are what used to be the dining and smoking rooms, visually linked together with mirrors and openings, overlooking the living room. Bedrooms and guest rooms were on the upper floors.

ADDRESS Na Cihlářce 10 / 2092, Praha 5 Smíchov
METRO Anděl – Line B
TRAM 4, 7, 9
BUS 137
ACCESS none

Smíchov to Hlubočepy

Adolf Loos and Karel Lhota (engineering) 1931–32

Adolf Loos and Karel Lhota (engineering) 1931–32

Villa Jíše

A stunning villa, situated under Děvín hill which commands excellent views of Prague valley towards the north-east. The three-storey building, entered at the raised ground-floor level, has a large double-height living room and dining room overlooked by a stair landing gallery at top-floor level. An external reinforced concrete spiral stair, reached from the dining room, leads into a steeply sloping garden, possibly inspired by a similar staircase used by Le Corbusier in Villa Ozenfant (1923). The top-floor terrace, with a canted-out solid balustrade with cut-out openings, was originally open, but has now been enclosed by windows.

The main structure is a reinforced concrete frame with 300 x 300 columns, infilled with hollow concrete blocks with interlocking ends which were cast on site. The whole building was rendered with white cement and fine marble chippings.

ADDRESS U Dívčích hradů 20 / 1905,
Praha 5 Smíchov
METRO Radlická – Line B
BUS 231
ACCESS none

Josef Havlíček and Karel Honzík 1929

Josef Havlíček and Karel Honzík 1929

Water Pressure Equalisation Tower

A 53-metre-high tower expressing its function clearly with three cylindrical water tanks grouped around a service staircase rising the full height of the structure. The staircase element is visible, exposed through cast glass channel cladding while the solid tube tanks are clad in pale blue and beige aluminium strips and topped by small copper-covered domes. The architecture of the entrance door at the foot of the tower borrows its formal language from Kotěra's Water Tower in Michle.

Once back down in the Vltava valley it is surprising how visible the tower is from a distance, becoming a landmark and a symbol of water technology.

Smíchov to Hlubočepy

ADDRESS Pražské vodárny, Tetínská, Praha 5 Radlice
METRO Radlická – Line B
BUS 231
ACCESS none

SIAL: Karel Hubáček and Zdeněk Patrman 1974–75

SIAL: Karel Hubáček and Zdeněk Patrman 1974–75

Barrandov Film Studios

Max Urban, as well as being an architect, was a film director and camer-aman. Together, with his actress wife Anna Sedláčková, he founded one of the first Czech film companies, asum, and wrote and shot films for the company before the First World War. In 1931, Urban proposed a complex of film studios at Barrandov designed purely on the functional require-ments for making and producing films.

The buildings are centred around two 20 x 32 metre studios, then judged an optimum size for film production. Attached to the studios are offices, development laboratories and copy production facilities including a preview cinema. The central tower, in addition to providing a focal point, is utilized for water storage. The studios are still used by the Czech film industry – proof of their good design and functionality.

ADDRESS Kříženeckého náměstí 5 / 322, Praha 5 Hlubočepy
BUS 105, 192, 246, 247, 248
ACCESS none

Max Urban 1931–34

Smíchov to Hlubočepy

Max Urban 1931–34

Villa, Barrandovská

There are a number of interesting luxury villas in this part of Prague. This one, by Vladimír Grégr, is a good example. Grégr was involved in the design of streamlined vehicles such as the Slovak Arrow railcar body made by the innovative automobile factory Tatra. This interest was transferred into his architecture, which picked up elements from transport technology. His buildings had rounded corners and smooth, sometimes wavy, façades producing aerodynamic forms that could almost move through the heavy Prague atmosphere.

Also by Vladimír Grégr are villas at Barrandovská 16 / 177 (1930–32), 17 / 444 (1939–41), 20 / 190 (1932), 25 / 307 (1936) and Skalní 10 / 327 (1932–33).

Smíchov to Hlubočepy

ADDRESS Barrandovská 46 / 180, Praha 5 Hlubočepy
BUS 105, 192, 246, 247, 248
ACCESS none

Vladimír Grégr 1931–32

Vladimír Grégr 1931–32

Barrandov Restaurant

A restaurant located in the glamorous setting of the Czech film industry where actors, actresses, directors and producers rested after long takes in the nearby studios. It was intended to woo Praguers to come to this spectacular setting on top of the lime rocks, named after a French geologist, J. Barrandov, high above the Vltava river. For a time it became busy: if you wanted to be somebody in Prague you had to appear on the terraces, with its backdrop of the proud white rendered building, and mingle with the famous. This era is long gone and the restaurant is fighting a battle with Prague's historical centre for occasional passing clientele.

Smíchov to Hlubočepy

ADDRESS Barrandovská 1 / 165, Praha 5 Hlubočepy
BUS 105, 192, 246, 247, 248
ACCESS open

Max Urban 1929, alterations by Vladimír Grégr 1939

Max Urban 1929, alterations by Vladimír Grégr 1939

Swimming Pool, Barrandov

Deep below the Barrandov restaurant lies a large swimming pool now overgrown with trees and shrubs establishing their roots into the crumbling concrete. The pool can be reached by a paved path from the restaurant starting on the left-hand side and leading down along the ridge of the rock.

The pool, the first national outdoor competition swimming stadium, was a large reinforced concrete structure filling a hollow at the bottom of the rock. The spectator seating was placed below the stone face at the western end. The concrete jumping tower is a most spectacular structure, with its simple form and stair winding around a single support column. The whole complex was designed by Václav Kolátor who after this experience, came to specialize in swimming pool projects.

The tower image was so photogenic that it became a symbol of its era and as such was used in a collage by Karel Teige (1941), a Devětsil founding member. It is good to see the starting blocks still there with their red numbers shining from under the moss.

ADDRESS Barrandovská 1 / 165, Praha 5
Hlubočepy
BUS 105, 192, 246, 247, 248
ACCESS open

Smíchov to Hlubočepy

Václav Kolátor 1929–30

Hradčany to Ruzyně

Villa Bílek 202
Hofmann & Stach Twin House 204
Villa Sucharda 206
Provincial Bank Apartment Building 208
Villa Gibian 210
French Schools 212
Baba Villas 214
Villa Barrová 220
Villa Linhart 222
Hotel Praha 224
Secondary School of Dr Beneš 226
Villa Traub 228
Villa Müller 230
Villa, U Ladronky 234
Old Prague Airport Terminal 236

Villa Bílek

František Bílek (1872–1941) was a Czech Secession painter and sculptor with expressionistic and symbolic tendencies. He stylised the human body, animals and plants, transforming them into ornamentality. Bílek turned to architecture in his most active period, realising that this form of creativity enhanced and embraced all other arts. He designed his own unusual villa and the neighbouring Villa Procházka (Mickiewiczova 3 / 234, 1910–11; see picture opposite). The design for Villa Bílek (pictured below) was based on a wheat field, where the concrete columns play the part of the ripe, half-grown or cut stems in contrast with the red earth of the brick walls and the trunks of trees surrounding the house.

Bílek's intention was to create an atelier which, at the same time, would become his art gallery. This building is one of the first flat roof constructions in Prague. In 1963, Bílek's wife gave the villa to the Prague Gallery of Art and three years later a permanent display of Bílek's work was arranged there.

Hradčany to Ruzyně

ADDRESS Mickiewiczova 1 / 233, Praha 6 Hradčany
METRO Hradčanská – Line A
TRAM 18, 22
ACCESS open 15 May–15 October, Tuesday–Sunday
10.00–12.00, 13.00–18.00

František Bílek 1910–11

František Bílek 1910–11

Hradčany to Ruzyně

Hofmann & Stach Twin House

A Cubist twin house arrangement with a static and solid appearance. Some movement is created by the 'spinning' cylinders enclosing the staircases and appearing in the bays above the porch entrances. Action is indicated by the windows rising with the pitch of the staircase. Gočár uses a Mansard roof to give the houses substance and weight. The massive short columns supporting the side bay of number 6 together with Cubist gargoyles at roof level and distorted metal bars on the windows at ground level are impressive.

Originally, the houses were surrounded by a purpose-built timber fence which reflected the Cubist design of the building. This has been replaced by a rather flimsy metal version. A delightful Cubist timber summer house still survives in the garden of number 4.

Hradčany to Ruzyně

ADDRESS Tychonova 4–6 / 268, 269,
Praha 6 Hradčany
METRO Hradčanská –Line A
TRAM 22
ACCESS none

Josef Gočár 1911–13

Josef Gočár 1911–13

Hradčany to Ruzyně

Villa Sucharda

There are a number of interesting villas around this small part of Bubeneč quarter. As well as Villa Sucharda, Slavíčkova boasts interesting houses at number 7 / 196 by Karel Mašek (1901), number 9 / 173 by Gustav Papež (1899) and number 17 / 153 by Jan Koula (1895–96). Around the corner at Suchardova 4 / 284 is a fairytale house (1907–08) by a Slovak architect, Dušan Jurkovič, and at Na Zátorce 3 / 289 the late Secessionist Villa Kraus by Emil Králíček and Matěj Blecha (1907–08).

Villa Sucharda, designed for the sculptor Stanislav Sucharda (1866–1916) towards the end of Secession, is well suited to his work and many examples are still scattered around the house and the garden. The villa itself is entered on a diagonal into a spacious hall with a staircase and gallery leading to the bedrooms at upper level. Off the hall is a dining room, with a semicircular bay window, and a salon also of semicircular shape with stained-glass windows. Between these two spaces is a smaller living room with a verandah facing the garden.

When built, the villa had a sculptor's studio attached on the west side which, in 1928, was separated and altered and is now a self-contained house. The original concave entrance gate decorated with sculptures has also been removed. The enclosing garden wall is typically modelled to the style of the villa, topped with yellow ceramic tiles, and has openings infilled with metal railings of a complementary design.

ADDRESS Slavíčkova 6 / 248, Praha 6 Bubeneč
METRO Hradčanská – Line A
TRAM 1, 8, 18, 25, 26
ACCESS none

Jan Kotěra 1905–07

Hradčany to Ruzyně

Jan Kotěra 1905–07

Provincial Bank Apartment Building

In May 1936 a competition was announced for a large apartment block for the Provincial Bank (Zemská banka). Podzemný's submission received the first prize and the opportunity to realise his scheme. The main seven-storey block faces the square, while the smaller six-storey side wings, with the last floor set back and a roof terrace shaded with pergolas, look onto the streets. There are 61 apartments of varying sizes, 15 shop units and 25 underground garages lit by rooflights set in the slab of the courtyard. A garden with tennis court and playground was also included in the project.

The building, constructed using a reinforced concrete frame, is faced in 65 x 300 mm Alit ceramic tiles and the underside of the balconies is clad in smaller 40 x 40 mm tiles. The block bends away from the line of the streets into the square and the partly recessed vertical lines of the balconies break the solid mass of the corners, contrasting with the horizontal bands of the windows. The large amount of glass used earned this building the name 'Glass Palace'.

ADDRESS Náměstí Svobody 1 / 728, Praha 6 Bubeneč
METRO Dejvická – Line A
TRAM 2, 20, 25, 26
ACCESS none

Richard F. Podzemný 1936–37

Richard F. Podzemný 1936–37

Villa Gibian

A volumetric design in the true Functionalist tradition with an attractive, vine-covered steel grid pergola over the entrance ramp. In 1923 Jaromír Krejcar, as an initiator and leading exponent of Czech modern architecture, supported the view that good architecture expresses externally the interior spaces. His large rooms were subdivided by furniture, moveable partitions and curtains rather than solid walls, similar to Miesian interiors, and were turned towards the sun and the garden. In the large Villa Gibian the service block is placed to the north, divided by the sloping access ramp from the main accommodation wing, which is modulated with balconies and terraces.

Hradčany to Ruzyně

ADDRESS Charlese de Gaulla 22 / 816, Praha 6 Bubeneč
METRO Dejvická – Line A
TRAM 2, 20, 25, 26
BUS 125
ACCESS none

Jaromír Krejcar 1927–29

Jaromír Krejcar 1927–29

French Schools

Twenty-seven-year-old Jan Gillar won a public architectural competition for this school project in 1931. The complex of schools, all of which used French as the teaching language, comprised a technical secondary school, an elementary school, a gymnasium and a kindergarten.

All the individual school buildings were meticulously designed, based on functional requirements, their form faithfully following the activities which were enclosed within. The kindergarten and gymnasium blocks connected directly with the playground and the garden while the specialised classrooms and study rooms formed a separate wing.

The classrooms were lit from windows on both sides, with smaller windows placed on the southern elevation. Terraces were provided at roof level for teaching in the open air.

ADDRESS Božkova 3 / 1784, Praha 6 Dejvice
METRO Dejvická – Line A
TRAM 20, 25
ACCESS none

Jan Gillar 1930–33

Jan Gillar 1930–33

Baba Villas

'The programme for the Baba exhibition is deliberately confined', Pavel Janák announced in 1931, 'to the one-family house, a dwelling type which is becoming more common in our country. The 30 exhibition houses will be constructed in a truly modern style, using new materials and structures. They will provide an overview of what a one-family house can and should be, and how contemporary living dictates its layout, situation and size, lighting, heating and the interior fixtures and fittings of individual rooms. The villas will be designed by architects who consider housing to be one of the most important tasks of our age. The exhibition will display an excellent survey of their efforts and will certainly contribute to stabilising and improving this housing type in our country and will provide moral stimulation.

'At Baba we shall build villas whose architects want to cooperate, shaping their design attitudes regarding grouping of buildings, their outlook, treatment of gardens and fencing and overall appearance. There is not always adequate mutual tolerance, taste and tact amongst new villa estates and only with an atmosphere of calmness can good neighbourliness be created!'

This permanent exhibition, finally increased to 33 villas, was devised and organised by Svaz československého díla (the Czechoslovak Decorative Arts Federation) and important Czech architects contributed their work. One foreigner was included – the Dutchman, Mart Stam whose design, together with those of Žák and Kučerová-Záveská, displayed most flair and skill in the handling of small building masses. The villas were specifically designed for clients who were members of the Svaz and leading personalities of Czech cultural life such as the painter and illustrator Cyril Bouda, historian Julius Glücklich, and painter and product designer Ladislav Sutnar.

Pavel Janák (overall concept) 1928–34

Individual villas:

Villa Košťál, Na ostrohu 41 / 1791, František Kerhart 1933–34
Villa Bouda, Na ostrohu 46 / 1712, Oldřich Starý 1932
Villa Dovolil, Na ostrohu 43 / 1797, Pavel Janák 1932
Villa Joska, Na ostrohu 48 / 1711, Jaroslav & Karel Fišer 1932
Villa Jíroušková, Na ostrohu 45 / 1796, František Kerhart, 1932–33
Villa Lisý, Na ostrohu 50 / 1710, A. Heythum & E. Linhart 1931–32
Villa Letošník, Na ostrohu 47 / 1795, František Kavalír 1932
Villa Vaváček, Na ostrohu 52 / 1709, Oldřich Starý 1931–32
Villa Suková, Na ostrohu 49 / 1794, Hana Kučerová-Záveská 1932
Villa Zaorálek, Na ostrohu 54 / 1708, Ladislav Žák 1931–32
Villa Čeněk, Na ostrohu 51 / 1793, Ladislav Žák 1931–32
Villa Řezáč, Na ostrohu 56 / 1707, Vojtěch Kerhart 1932
Villa Zadák, Na ostrohu 53 / 1792, František Zelenka 1934
Villa Peřina, Na ostrohu 58 / 1706, František Kerhart 1933
Villa Lom, Na Babě 1 / 1783, Josef Gočár 1935–36
Villa Herain, Na Babě 3 / 1782, Ladislav Žák 1931–32
Villa Bautz, Na Babě 4 / 1799, František Kerhart 1933
Villa Balling, Na Babě 5 / 1781, Hana Kučerová-Záveská 1931–32
Villa Lindová, Na Babě 6 / 1800, Pavel Janák 1933–34
Villa Heřman, Na Babě 7 / 1780, Oldřich Starý 1931–32
Villa Moravcová, Na Babě 8 / 1801, Vojtěch Kerhart 1933–34
Villa Palička, Na Babě 9 / 1779, Mart Stam & Jiří Palička 1931–32
Villa Spíšek, Na Babě 11 / 1777, Ladislav Machoň 1932–33
Villa Poláček, Na Babě 12 / 1803, Jan E. Koula 1933–34
Villa Uhlíř, Na Babě 13 / 1776, František Kavalír 1932
Villa Glücklich, Jarní 3 / 1798, Josef Gočár 1933–34

Pavel Janák (overall concept) 1928–34

Pavel Janák (overall concept) 1928–34

Villa Janák, Nad Paťankou 16 / 1785, Pavel Janák 1931–32
Villa Maule, Nad Paťankou 18 / 1786, Josef Gočár 1931–32
Villa Kytlica, Nad Paťankou 22 / 1788, Josef Gočár 1932–33
Villa Bělehrádek, Nad Paťankou 24 / 1789, F. Kerhart, 1935–36
Villa Sutnar, Průhledová 2 / 1790, Oldřich Starý 1932
Villa Lužná, Průhledová 6 / 1804, Zdeněk Blažek 1931–33
Villa Munk, Průhledová 10 / 1705, Josef Fuchs 1932

ADDRESS Na ostrohu, Na Babě,
Nad Paťankou, Jarní, Průhledová,
Praha 6 Dejvice
TRAM 20, 25
BUS 107, 116, 125, 131, 147, 160
ACCESS none

Pavel Janák (overall concept) 1928–34

Villa Barrová

Another analogy from the brilliant Žák where the two principal elevations offer different approaches. The east side has a rounded end, a large terrace in front of the living room and stair to the garden, a balcony on the bedroom floor projecting out of the façade and a rounded screen on the roof terrace turned towards Prague (this elevation can be seen from Na Míčance). The plain, almost windowless façade pointed towards the street hides an internal staircase, with a deep cut on the left side giving visitors a glimpse of the coming view once on the balcony or the roof terrace. The funnel-like chimney projecting above the roof line and the small circular windows are reminiscent of a steamboat.

Also look at Villa Verunáč (1931) at Neherovská 10 / 1522 by Josef Chochol, a rectilinear, straightforward building somehow missing the subtlety and play of forms of Žák's design.

ADDRESS Neherovská 8 / 677, Praha 6 Dejvice
BUS 125, 131
ACCESS none

Ladislav Žák 1937

Hradčany to Ruzyně

Ladislav Žák 1937

Villa Linhart

One of the best examples of Functionalist architecture in Prague. Designed and built by the architect, Evžen Linhart, for himself, Villa Linhart is L-shaped in plan with void and solid volumes complementing each of the wings; a solid on the ground floor to the right reflects a void on the left and this arrangement is reversed on the floor above. The voids are indicated by overhangs or by extension of the main structure framing the space. The windows are perfectly positioned, their size skilfully chosen in proportion to the area of surrounding walls, generating an abstracted composition.

On the lower ground floor there are service spaces, a kitchen, laundry and garage. The ground floor accommodates the living room with a ramp to the dining area and a studio. The top floor contains the bedrooms and a roof terrace is reached by a stair on the side elevation. The villa was furnished with built-in bookcases, wardrobes, beds, tables and chairs in tubular steel frame; some chairs were in bentwood. A dumb waiter was installed between the kitchen and dining room.

Jan Rosůlek's villa is at Na viničních horách 44 / 773 (1927–29). It was reconstructed by Vladimír Grégr in 1939.

ADDRESS Na viničních horách 46 / 774, Praha 6 Dejvice
METRO Dejvická – Line A
TRAM 2, 20, 26
BUS 125, 131
ACCESS none

Hradčany to Ruzyně

Evžen Linhart 1927–29

Evžen Linhart 1927–29

Hotel Praha

This luxury hotel was built for the use of the leading members of the Czechoslovak Communist Party to entertain foreign guests and high-ranking party officials visiting from fraternal communist countries. The intention was to show the skills that Czech industry and culture could offer and no money was spared. The surprising location of this large building in a residential suburb was justified by fabulous panoramic views from public areas as well as the guest rooms.

The design concept is based on extending the hill's contours into the wavy form of the building. The planting on the continuous balconies reinforces this idea. The overhang above the south terrace acts as a shading device but also as a security barrier separating the guest rooms from the public areas. The north elevation is severe, forbidding and uninviting, the vertical access elements reminiscent of watch towers. The hotel's past is chillingly revealed by the remnants of electrified fencing which used to surround the whole estate.

ADDRESS Sušická 20 / 2450, Praha 6 Dejvice
METRO Dejvická – Line A
TRAM 2, 20, 26
ACCESS open

Jaroslav Paroubek, Radko Černý and Arnošt Navrátil 1975–81

Secondary School of Dr Beneš

A simple but effective and purposeful building unfortunately placed too close to the busy Evropská. This L-shaped school, Linhart's favourite arrangement, spreads upwards into a six- and seven-storey high structure. The entrance block extended towards Evropská is the most modelled with a slanting roof hiding a recessed top floor which is covered on the longer wing with a projecting roof. The entrance is signalled by a reinforced concrete canopy with large openings above glazed with glass blocks. Some buildings make demands on your emotions – this one is too smooth to have that effect.

Hradčany to Ruzyně

ADDRESS Evropská 33 / 330, Praha 6 Dejvice
METRO Dejvická – Line A
TRAM 2, 20, 26
ACCESS none

Evžen Linhart 1937–38

Villa Traub

A rather grand villa situated on a difficult sloping site between the lively Milady Horákové and the steep Pod hradbami. Edmund Traub was a leather manufacturer who invited Bruno Paul from Berlin to design a large family residence and solve the problem of the site, with a 12-metre difference in levels. Paul set the villa into the slope, giving the street a four-storey elevation against a three-storey long horizontal face into the garden.

The rectangular stone-faced façade contrasts with the neighbouring houses, clearly standing out with its cool and ordered architecture. The Traub family used the villa for ten years before fleeing, in 1938, when the German Reich occupied Sudetenland. Since then it has been used as diplomatic quarters by a number of east European countries.

In 1992 the building was reconstructed for the Delegation of the Commission of the European Communities. Parts of the interior are preserved, including the entrance hall, a well-formed main staircase with a fine balustrade, built-in furniture, mirrors and purpose-designed iron-mongery. The garden was also renovated to the original design recreating, as Paul termed it, an additional garden room.

ADDRESS Pod hradbami 17 / 658,
Praha 6 Střešovice
TRAM 1, 2, 8, 18, 25, 26
ACCESS none

Bruno Paul 1928–29, renovated by Ladislav Kalivoda 1992

Hradčany to Ruzyně

Bruno Paul 1928–29, renovated by Ladislav Kalivoda 1992

Villa Müller

Adolf Loos designed this villa within a few weeks of being commissioned by František Müller. Müller, who was a partner in the Kapsa & Müller construction firm, negotiated the building permit with the local authority. Permission was granted on appeal after several attempts as the villa's footprint was larger than permitted and the intricate interior layout did not clearly follow the allowable two-storey height limit.

This villa is a plain and unassuming building from the outside and on approaching one wonders what all the fuss is about. The windows seem too small to allow enough light to the interior. In fact the exterior confirms Adolf Loos's determination 'not to build a beautiful house but a house with a simple roof and simple windows'.

But what a revelation once inside. The spaces are just the right size, and the windows let the correct quantity of sunlight in to set the villa alight. Interwoven rooms partly overlooking each other, yet secluded enough to provide privacy, are carved out of the cubic volume and connected together with a central staircase which serves all levels and spreads with a few steps into all the major rooms.

Entering each space, you are confounded by the three-dimensional complexity of the layout; it is difficult to establish where you are in relation to the rest of the villa. Colourful finishes of cipollino de Sion marble, Silesian syenite granite, lemonwood, maple, oak and mahogany hardwoods, Opaxit glass, ceramic and Delft tiles, curtain fabrics, mirrors, carpets, polished parquet floors, leather upholstery, and purpose-designed light fittings and ironmongery give richness to the whole experience. Here Loos exchanged the decoration of the past for something more magnificent. 'Rich materials and good workmanship should not only be considered as making up for lack of decoration but as far surpassing it in sumptuousness. Noble materials are a gift from God!'

Adolf Loos and Karel Lhota (engineering) 1928–30

Adolf Loos and Karel Lhota (engineering) 1928–30

Hradčany to Ruzyně

From the roof terrace is another view of Prague, this time confined by the extended side walls. The wall on the right has a large opening to frame the view of St Vitus Cathedral.

This remarkable creation is an architectural jack-in-a-box and there is no other building like it in Prague or possibly anywhere else. Loos's belief was that space was something to be experienced, and on leaving the villa one genuinely feels exhausted from the mental effort required to appreciate all the qualities of this exceptional 20th century architectural masterpiece.

Villa Müller is true to Loos's notion that 'a building should be dumb on the outside and reveal its wealth only on the inside'.

ADDRESS Nad hradním vodojemem
14 / 642, Praha 6 Střešovice
TRAM 1, 2, 18
ACCESS to be opened after restoration

Adolf Loos and Karel Lhota (engineering) 1928–30

Adolf Loos and Karel Lhota (engineering) 1928–30

Villa, U Ladronky

A handsome villa perfectly positioned on a corner site in a quiet residential suburb. Smetana studied under Janák and Gočár and, in 1926, became a member of Devětsil. From simple Functionalist elements Smetana developed more plastic shapes and forms sometimes of abstract, subjective origins. This depth of his approach is perceptible in this sensitively handled villa with carefully proportioned volumes and façades of sculptural quality.

ADDRESS U Ladronky 31 / 1334, Praha 6 Břevnov
TRAM 8, 22
ACCESS none

Pavel Smetana 1938–39

Pavel Smetana 1938–39

Old Prague Airport Terminal

These buildings were built to replace Kbely Airport, which could not cope with the growth in air traffic. The group of buildings consists of a terminal, cargo and administration facility, air traffic control tower, three hangers, plantroom and apartment blocks for staff all enclosed by a perimeter fence with an entry guard house. The terminal, with its shallow arched segmented roof, corresponds well with the control tower, with rounded corners clad in glass, and adjacent buildings faced in ceramic tiles.

The airport buildings came into service in April 1937 and are still in use as an overflow facility for special flights, VIPs and state visits. The main airport terminal, further west, was designed by Karel Bubeníček, Karel Filsák, Jiří Louda, and Jan Šrámek and built between 1964 and 1968. With additional business and tourist travel to Prague since 1989 the Ruzyně airport terminal is being extended to include the modern equipment and accommodation required by late-20th century travellers.

Between the two airport terminals is an interesting aircraft maintenance hanger with a cable-suspended roof structure designed by Vladimír Conk, Karel Hubáček and Jiří Lášek, also built between 1964 and 1968.

ADDRESS K letišti 2 / 550, 533 Praha 6 Ruzyně
BUS 108, 119, 179
ACCESS restricted

Adolf Benš 1932–34, Kamil Roškot (Guard House) 1934–35

Adolf Benš 1932–34, Kamil Roškot (Guard House) 1934–35

Holešovice to Troja

Josef Hlávka Bridge (Hlávkův most) **240**
Tennis Stadium **242**
Electricity Company Building **244**
Apartment Building, Schnirchova **246**
Prague Trade Fair Palace **248**
Apartment Building, Kamenická **250**
Retail, Cinema and Apartment Buildings **252**
Winklerová Retail and Apartment Building **254**
Apartment Building, Čechova **256**
Molochov Apartment Buildings **258**
Apartment Building, Letohradská **260**
National Technical Museum (Národní technické museum) **262**
Restaurant Praha Expo 58 **264**
Villa, Trojská **266**
Villa Chytilová **268**

Josef Hlávka Bridge (Hlávkův most)

A bridge named after an architect, benefactor and first president of the Czech Academy of Fine Arts, Josef Hlávka (1831–1908). It has been built in different styles and materials, the southern end in steel and the northern section in concrete. The most interesting is the middle part spanning across Štvanice Island. The wavy edge gives a hint of Cubism and a dynamic quality to the otherwise static structure. Between the arches over each pier, niches filled with statues by Jan Štursa are formed within the concrete, punctuated by a raised square pattern. Round sculpted emblems above the piers on the northern part of the bridge are of the past mayors of Prague by Otto Gutfreund.

The steel bridge was rebuilt in concrete between 1958 and 1962 and the whole structure widened to 28 metres by building another concrete bridge to the east side which imitated all the original details and sculptural decorations.

ADDRESS continuation of Bubenská, Praha 7 Holešovice
METRO Vltavská – Line c
TRAM 3, 8
ACCESS open

Pavel Janák and František Mencl (engineering) 1909–12

Pavel Janák and František Mencl (engineering) 1909–12

Tennis Stadium

This island on the River Vltava is called Štvanice (Chase) because, until the early 19th century, fights took place between dogs, deer, bulls and bears in a wooden amphitheatre. This cruel entertainment was stopped in 1815 and replaced by public bars, a circus and frequent air balloon displays. In 1901, the first tennis courts were laid here for the Czech Lawn Tennis Club (founded in 1893). In 1926 a large central court with seating was built to stage tournament matches and the new structure has now replaced this.

The central court, with a seating capacity of 7000, splits into several wing elements which are divided formally by access staircases. The main public approach ramp rises to the first-floor level over the top of the changing cabins and players' accommodation, separating the two areas. The court sits elegantly in the natural setting of the island. The subdued colours of the grey and silver structure, together with the play of shadows and light, underline the sculptural form of the steelwork. This is a fitting setting from which Czech tennis champions assault the rest of the world.

ADDRESS Ostrov Štvanice, Praha 7 Holešovice
METRO Vltavská – Line C
TRAM 3, 8
ACCESS open

Josef Káleš and Jana Novotná 1982–86

Holešovice to Troja

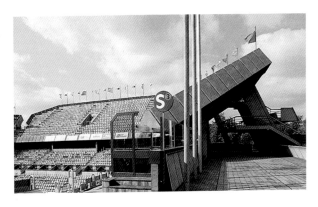

Josef Káleš and Jana Novotná 1982–86

Electricity Company Building

A well-designed group of buildings which came about as the result of a limited architectural competition in which the winning team decided to build centrally on the site rather than around its perimeter. The main part of the development is an eight-storey building containing an impressive full-height central entrance hall. Surrounded by access galleries, it is lit from above and by a large west-facing glazed wall and is equipped with a staircase and paternoster lifts, very popular in Prague, leading to all the floors. To this hub six- and three-storey blocks are attached. Public baths and a lecture theatre were originally located in the basement.

This was one of the first buildings in Prague that was clad externally in ceramic tiles. The complex of buildings evokes the brisk efficiency of a smooth, well-oiled engine but also of the Big Brother of technology watching closely over the hard-working staff.

ADDRESS Bubenská 1 / 1477, Praha 7 Holešovice
METRO Vltavská – Line C
TRAM 1, 8, 25, 26
ACCESS none

Adolf Benš and Josef Kříž 1927–35

Adolf Benš and Josef Kříž 1927–35

Apartment Building, Schnirchova

An apartment building with continuous bands of windows contained in a projecting bay and supported on either side by single balconies with a mesh-type balustrade, a favourite detail of Rosenberg. His buildings, though plain, are well detailed. It is a pleasure to find the simplicity and elegance of wired glass balustrades with thin timber handrails to the main staircase together with landings paved in glass blocks. Rosenberg used a similar design in his arcade building, Štěpánská – Ve Smečkách, Praha 1 Nové Město.

ADDRESS Schnirchova 29 / 1084,
Praha 7 Holešovice
METRO Vltavská – Line C
TRAM 5, 12, 17
ACCESS none

Eugene Rosenberg 1935–37

Prague Trade Fair Palace

The result of an architectural competition for a trade fair building announced in 1924 gave Tyl the first prize and placed Fuchs third. Both architects were persuaded to combine ideas from their initial proposals and prepare a joint design which, when completed, became one of the most progressive public buildings in Czechoslovakia.

The heart of the building is a large internal atrium, whose floor was used for the main displays, surrounded by exhibition spaces with wide access galleries. Under the entrance hall was a cinema and at the top floor a restaurant and a café adjacent to the roof terrace. The structure is in reinforced concrete which allowed for full-length continuous windows wrapping around the sharp corners.

The Prague trade exhibitions ended in 1951 when they were transferred to Brno. Since then the building has been used as administrative offices for various state enterprise firms. After a devastating fire on 14 August 1974 the building was renovated and converted by SIAL to the National Gallery of Modern Art with some additional business premises. It is a very fitting piece of architecture which complements objects of modern art and becomes a showpiece itself.

In 1928 Le Corbusier noted: 'I congratulate Prague and local architecture on being able to realise such a grandiose work. Seeing the Trade Fair Palace, I understood how to make large buildings, having so far built only several relatively small houses on a low budget'.

ADDRESS Dukelských hrdinů 47 / 530, Praha 7 Holešovice
METRO Vltavská – Line C
TRAM 5, 12, 17
ACCESS open Tuesday to Sunday 10.00–18.00, Thursday 10.00–21.00

Oldřich Tyl and Josef Fuchs 1924–28

Holešovice to Troja

Holešovice to Troja

Oldřich Tyl and Josef Fuchs 1924–28

Apartment Building, Kamenická

A dark and mysterious building demanding reverence and humble admiration from passers-by. Its Rondo-Cubist elements create a play of shadow and form. Are the spaces between the windows niches or convex forms? From a distance it is hard to decide. The ground-floor columns with their cone heads seem just able to manage to support the monumental weight of the façade crushing down from above. Here the typical bright colours of Rondo-Cubism give way to a more sober but dignified offering. Novotný surprises all the time by producing unequalled masterpieces in each style he creatively adopted.

ADDRESS Kamenická 35 / 811, Praha 7 Holešovice
METRO Vltavská – Line C
TRAM 1, 8, 25, 26
ACCESS none

Holešovice to Troja

Otakar Novotný 1923–24

Retail, Cinema and Apartment Buildings

A large block incorporating shops and offices along Milady Horákové with apartments and a cinema called Oko (Eye) entered from Františka Křižíka. Most interesting is the treatment of the round corner, laced with horizontal balconies and crowned with a roof terrace. The whole corner device lightens the bulk of the building and broadcasts its presence from a long way down the hill.

ADDRESS Františka Křižíka 11–15 / 460, 461, Praha 7 Holešovice
METRO Vltavská – Line C
TRAM 1, 8, 25, 26
ACCESS ground floor and cinema open

Jaroslav Stockar-Bernkopf and Josef Šolc 1938–39

Holešovice to Troja

Jaroslav Stockar-Bernkopf and Josef Šolc 1938–39

Winklerová Retail and Apartment Building

A solution to an unusual urban site, in the shape of a parallelogram. It is set back from the neighbouring building façades creating increased pavement area at the front which is used for free-standing advertising and display cases. The shape of the site gives the building sharp corners, particularly noticeable on the rear elevation. The combination of window openings, balconies, narrow recesses, small canopy projections and the top floor setbacks results in a pleasant composition. The distorted geometry of the internal and external spaces and volumes produces an unusual juxtaposition of forms not normally encountered in buildings of this kind and period.

Also look at the retail and apartment building by Eugene Rosenberg (1937), at Milady Horákové 56 / 387, Praha 7 Holešovice.

ADDRESS Milady Horákové 63 / 386, Praha 7 Holešovice
METRO Vltavská – Line C
TRAM 1, 8, 25, 26
ACCESS ground floor open

Karel Janů 1938–39

Karel Janů 1938–39

Apartment Building, Čechova

Roškot's apartment building signifies the beginning of a new modern approach to architecture after the late Cubist extravaganza and the arrival of the Purist movement. Roškot also built on the experience of Kotěra's Modernism before the First World War. The façade is divided into simple rectangles, without decoration, with only render and brickwork used as external materials. The large window on the ground floor was originally divided into three vertical openings with solid piers in between. Deep in the entrance is a wall-mounted sculpture of the Bricklayer, by Otto Gutfreund.

ADDRESS Čechova 29 / 587, Praha 7 Bubeneč
TRAM 1, 8, 25, 26
ACCESS none

Kamil Roškot 1923–24

Kamil Roškot 1923–24

Molochov Apartment Buildings

A 252-metre-long continuous block of apartments, with shops at ground level, consisting of 14 houses individually designed by a group of seven architects. The overall seven-floor composition of the block as well as two of the units was designed by Josef Havlíček.

The long elevation is lightened by loggias rhythmically subdividing the solid parts. The top floor is set back on both sides providing roof terraces and is interrupted only by staircases at the back. The plan of the apartments is, typically, divided into three zones: a living room facing the Letná Plain, an internal hall with glazed doors and screens, and kitchen, bathroom and access staircases at the rear. The apartments vary in size from a studio flat to ten-room units. The external finishes are long lasting and good quality: ceramic tiles, marble, travertine and render. Most windows have built-in timber slatted awnings.

Individual buildings: Otto and Karel Kohn (72, 84–90, 96), Arnošt Mühlstein and Viktor Fürth (74, 94), František Votava (92), Leo Lauermann (76–78), Josef Havlíček (80–82).

ADDRESS Milady Horákové 72–96 / 845–862, Praha 7 Holešovice
METRO Hradčanská – Line A
TRAM 1, 8, 25, 26
ACCESS none

Josef Havlíček 1936–38 (overall concept)

Holešovice to Troja

Josef Havlíček 1936–38 (overall concept)

Apartment Building, Letohradská

This block was built as an infill between existing buildings which dictated its depth and height. The concrete frame structure is faced with grey glazed Alit tiles which are bordered by a pale yellow band of mosaic tiles to define the limit of the whole composition against the neighbouring buildings. Popular timber slatted awnings shade the windows from the afternoon sun. The balustrades to the small end loggias are constructed in cast glass blocks.

Originally a statue of a girl by Marta Jirásková stood by the entrance but was only there for a short time. During the war, the owner of the building was worried that the Nazis would confiscate the sculpture and it was removed.

Holešovice to Troja

ADDRESS Letohradská 60 / 760, Praha 7
Holešovice
METRO Vltavská – Line C
TRAM 1, 8, 25, 26
ACCESS none

Josef Havlíček 1938–39

Josef Havlíček 1938–39

National Technical Museum (Národní technické museum)

The exterior gives the impression of a rather grim and precise building. However, the main exhibition hall is exhilarating with its glass-block paved galleries and steel roof, whose structural form follows the natural stress lines.

As well as the building, the exhibits, which celebrate the innovative skills of Czech engineers and designers, are worth seeing. Collections include superb streamlined Tatra and Škoda passenger cars, racing cars and locomotives displayed on the main floor of the hall, and motorbikes and bicycles placed along the galleries. Aeroplanes are attractively suspended in mid-flight from the building structure. An air balloon embedded in the roof adds to the atmosphere of the space.

ADDRESS Kostelní 42–44 / 1300, 1320, Praha 7 Holešovice
METRO Vltavská – Line c
TRAM 5, 12, 14, 17, 26
ACCESS open Tuesday–Sunday 9.00–17.00

Milan Babuška 1937–40

Holešovice to Troja

Milan Babuška 1937–40

Restaurant Praha Expo 58

Czech architects were successful with the Czechoslovak exhibition pavilion at Expo 58 held in Brussels. Their proposal received a gold medal and two diplomas for the best architectural design and exhibition display. After the Expo, it was decided to bring the building back to Prague and rebuild the main pavilion in the grounds of the Exhibition Centre, originally set up for the 1891 Jubilee Exhibition held at Stromovka. In 1991 the pavilion was destroyed by fire.

Part of the Brussels pavilion was an independent restaurant building which served a selection of Czech food and drink to Expo visitors. The restaurant was also brought back and re-erected in Letenské sady (Letná Orchards) in an attractive position on the cliffs above the Vltava, with fabulous views over Prague. The building is curved in plan and the main restaurant is at first-floor level, exploiting the view, with a comfortable terrace bar stretching below at ground level. The façades are simply but effectively faced in glass and aluminium cladding. A small blue-tiled pool with a statue completes the landscaped setting.

ADDRESS Letenské sady 1500, Praha 7 Holešovice
METRO Vltavská – Line C
TRAM 5, 12, 14, 17, 26
ACCESS under restoration

František Cubr, Josef Hrubý and Zdeněk Pokorný 1957–60

Villa, Trojská

A classic Functionalist building by Adolf Benš, designer of the Electricity Company Building, constructed in a reinforced concrete frame with reinforced concrete floors and roof. The steel reinforcement in the slabs was laid diagonally. External walls have a layer of insulation sandwiched between the two skins of brickwork. Windows were double-glazed, sliding and folding in metal with timber cores. The external render was made up of a finely ground marble and cement mixture with a cement outer layer removed by rubbing with carborundum.

The inclusion of a tree, enclosed by the extended structural frame of the building, in the architectural composition, adds the functional requirement of bringing the human habitat closer to nature.

ADDRESS Trojská 134 / 224, Praha 7 Troja
BUS 112
ACCESS none

Adolf Benš 1928–30

Adolf Benš 1928–30

Villa Chytilová

This white modern villa, with a multitude of spaces, levels and external terraces, sits on the edge of a hill overlooking Troja Castle and the Zoological Gardens with Prague to the south. It is certainly a stunning and suitable location for the home of the film director, Věra Chytilová. Her films, O něčem jiném (*About Something Else*; 1963) and *Sedmikrásky* (*Daisies*; 1966), became known worldwide and helped to establish an excellent reputation for Czech cinematography of that time.

Emil Přikryl continued the tradition of Prague's villa architecture by choosing white rendered surfaces, flat roofs and large glazed windows projecting into the rich planting of the hilltop garden. A small external swimming pool completes all the needs and comforts of this secluded idyl of late-20th century living.

ADDRESS Pod Havránkou 22 / 619, Praha 7 Troja
BUS 112
ACCESS none

Emil Přikryl 1970–75

Emil Přikryl 1970–75

Ďáblice to Hostivař

Cemetery Entrance Pavilions, Entrance Gate and Perimeter Wall 272
Bulovka Hospital Dermatology Pavilion 274
Water Tower and Airport Lighthouse 276
Villa Hain 278
Primary and Secondary Schools 280
Villa Kotěra 282
Hussite Congregation Church and Apartment Building 284
Pragobanka Development 286
Church of St Wenceslas 288
Bakery 290

Cemetery Entrance Pavilions, Entrance Gate and Perimeter Wall

A partly realised project for the Ďáblice cemetery was the only Cubist work in Prague by Vlatislav Hofman despite many scheme proposals, including the Palacký Square reconstruction and the Žižka Monument competition at Vítkov Hill. The cemetery project should have included a mortuary, a crematorium, a ceremonial hall and administrative offices but only two entrance pavilions with an enclosing perimeter wall and the main gates were built. Nevertheless, the mastery of the architect is clearly evident. The pavilion's stepped copper roof topped with a lantern, the eight-sided bulging windows together with the strongly modelled metal-work gates and crystal forms inserted into the perimeter wall show confidence and a delicate skill in dealing with Cubist forms.

Ďáblice to Hostivař

ADDRESS Ďáblické hřbitovy, Ďáblická, Praha 8 Ďáblice
TRAM 12, 17, 24
BUS 103, 136, 258
ACCESS open

Vlatislav Hofman 1912–13

Vlastislav Hofman 1912–13

Bulovka Hospital Dermatology Pavilion

An interesting group of buildings consisting of a small isolation ward block and higher dermatology pavilion beyond. The architecture of the isolation ward displays two different faces: one with roof parapet, balcony edges and balustrades parallel with the street, and the other in which individual wards looking into the sun and towards the river step, creating a saw-like edge on each floor.

The sienna-coloured taller building behind is divided into three distinct vertical sections, each resolved differently. The block has two set-back levels with balconies at the top framed by end walls. The middle section has unusually cut window slots with rounded ends which follow the pitch of the staircase inside, adding dynamic expression to the composition. On the right is a bay section standing on two exposed columns with glass block infill to openings above. This is a masterly set of buildings which is attractive from every angle and holds together despite its diversity.

ADDRESS view from Bulovka, Praha 8 Libeň
TRAM 12, 14, 24
ACCESS none

Jan Rosůlek 1935–36

Ďáblice to Hostivař

Jan Rosúlek 1935–36

Water Tower and Airport Lighthouse

Kbely was the first Prague airport and was used from October 1923 for flights between Prague and Bratislava by Letecký dopravní oddíl (Airline Transport Division) and from 1924 by the Czechoslovak Air Service Co. and Czechoslovak State Airways. In 1928 a flight from London to Prague cost ten pounds and three shillings, and took over 12 hours via Rotterdam, Essen, Kassel and Marienbad (Mariánské Lázně). Brave air travellers were advised that cotton wool was distributed to lessen the roar of the engines and propeller and that luncheon baskets could be obtained at the aerodrome restaurant but, for an initial trip, it was wiser to depend upon a few dry biscuits and a little fruit. A tough deal for a 12-hour flight!

The lighthouse and water tower at Kbely is 43 metres high. There are at least ten other similar water towers in Prague including the Radlice tower (page 190) and Michle tower (page 174). At present, Kbely is a military airfield used by the Czech Army and no access is possible, though the tower can be seen well from the public road.

Ďáblice to Hostivař

ADDRESS Mladoboleslavská, Praha 9 Kbely
BUS 110, 185, 201, 259, 278
ACCESS none

Otakar Novotný 1924

Otakar Novotný 1924

Villa Hain

This small building, built for an aircraft engineer, is another of Ladislav Žák's masterpieces. It is situated on an elevated position overlooking Kbely Plain, where Prague's main airport used to be situated.

The form of the building, with its sun-bathing terrace, is reminiscent of an aeroplane body and includes a roof observation platform provided at the request of the owner. The terrace at first-floor level could be surrounded by blinds, concealed when not in use in an overhanging frame. The structure is of reinforced concrete, rendered over steel mesh, and was sprayed originally with a pale beige colour wash. Windows were steel with timber cores.

Regrettably, the structure housing the terrace blinds has been removed and the villa is surrounded closely by mature trees making it difficult to appreciate fully its unusual form. The view from the observation platform is now obscured by neighbouring villas.

ADDRESS Na vysočanských vinicích 31 / 404, Praha 9 Vysočany
metro Českomoravská – Line B
TRAM 8, 19
BUS 151, 181
ACCESS none

Ďáblice to Hostivař

Ladislav Žák 1932–33

Ladislav Žák 1932–33

Primary and Secondary Schools

An accomplished group of white-tiled buildings, with circular and continuous windows, designed by Vladimír Frýda, an architect mainly involved in school projects. The taller secondary school block accommodates a large entrance hall with a main staircase leading to all the floors and from which the classrooms are reached. This space, quiet during lessons, comes alive at break times with pupils meeting each other in one vertical circulation area through which everyone has to pass.

The lower block to the east has a canteen and houses the primary school. The schools are set on the edge of a park which makes the morning walk to the school or the journey home at the end of the day pleasant and relaxing.

ADDRESS Špitalská 2 / 700, 789, Praha 9 Vysočany
METRO Českomoravská – Line B
TRAM 8, 19
ACCESS none

Vladimír Frýda 1927–37

Vladimír Frýda 1927–37

Villa Kotěra

An important villa, designed in the brief interlude between the end of the Secession period and the rise of Cubist creativity, in a rational Modernism style. This approach is apparent by the distinct expression of the internal volumes externally and the use of brickwork in combination with render for external finishes.

Here in Jan Kotěra's own villa the entrance, the main staircase and living areas are defined as separate elements but are put together in a simple and effective asymmetrical composition. The use of decoration is reduced to a minimum and the forms, volumes and materials provide all that is required to define the architectural composition.

ADDRESS Hradešínská 6 / 1542,
Praha 10 Vinohrady
METRO Jiřího z Poděbrad – Line A
TRAM 4, 16, 22
ACCESS none

Jan Kotěra 1908–09

Hussite Congregation Church and Apartment Building

Two buildings are placed together, an apartment building adjacent to an evangelical church with a stand-alone tall square tower. For part of its height the tower encloses a spiral staircase and is topped with a copper chalice, a symbol of Czech Protestant religion. The staircase has been used as a dynamic element providing additional vertical direction to the tower, like a giant corkscrew. Render finish is applied to the apartments and the church, and is further enhanced by rough-hewn stone slabs in parts enclosing the ground level. Surprisingly, one slab sticks out of the plane of the church façade near the foot of the tower.

ADDRESS Dykova 1 / 51, Praha 10 Vinohrady
METRO Jiřího z Poděbrad – Line A
TRAM 16
ACCESS none

Pavel Janák 1931–33

Ďáblice to Hostivař

Pavel Janák 1931–33

Ďáblice to Hostivař

Pragobanka Development

This is a new project from one of the Czech avant-garde architectural practices led in the 1960s and 1970s by Karel Hubáček who taught a number of current leading Czech architects in his studio. After Hubáček's retirement in 1989 Jiří Suchomel was left in charge of SIAL. The Pragobanka scheme shows that SIAL's fresh approach has not weakened and that it still is one of the most talented architectural groups in the country.

The existing bank administrative building remains and is connected to the new development by a glazed high-level canopy stretched over an entrance courtyard. The new buildings start with a rounded form on the corner of Vinohradská and Starostrašnická advertising the development. The southern block, with its wavy façade, entices pedestrians to walk along, drawing them towards the facilities provided. The buildings are clad in stone, glass and aluminium. The design echoes the high-tech style and has a hint of Deconstructivism. It is certainly a better offering and way forward than the early 1990s Post-modernist fever which seems to have affected most other Czech architects.

ADDRESS Vinohradská 230, Praha 10 Strašnice
METRO Strašnická – Line A
TRAM 7, 11, 19, 26
ACCESS bank premises open

SIAL: Radim Kousal, Petr Kincl and collective 1993–95

SIAL: Radim Kousal, Petr Kincl and collective 1993–95

Church of St Wenceslas

A large church which is set into a steep slope of the green square of the Vršovice suburb. The tall church clock tower rises from the wide entrance space dividing it in half and making its presence known to the worshippers. The monumental but simple central nave has a roof plane which steps up as it follows the slope of the ground outside.

Daylight is cast towards the altar through rooflights inserted between the stepped roof planes. The nave is round-ended with eight tall vertical windows letting more light into the focal point of the church. The windows are decorated with a stained-glass design of St Wenceslas by a sculptor and designer, Josef Kaplický (1899–1962). On the main altar is a large cross by Čeněk Vosmík.

ADDRESS Náměstí Svatopluka Čecha, Praha 10 Vršovice
TRAM 4, 6, 7, 22, 24
ACCESS open during services

Josef Gočár 1928–33

Josef Gočár 1928–33

Bakery

An example of Prague industrial architecture. Despite having been built after the First World War, in the design of this bakery Bohumil Hypšman followed Kotěra's Modernism established in the first decade of the century. Hypšman was a traditionalist and slow to accept modern trends which others adopted so eagerly.

The complex includes a factory and administrative buildings and an unusually designed silo. The decorative motifs are taken through all the buildings, but are most prominent on the silo, where the form of the containers changes at the top to a rectangular mass animated with geometric squares and circular windows.

ADDRESS U továren 27 / 261 Praha 10 Hostivař
TRAIN Praha Hostivař
TRAM 22, 26
BUS 101, 111, 122, 240
ACCESS none

Bohumil Hypšman 1919–22

Bohumil Hypšman 1919–22

Biographies

Adolf Benš
18 May 1894 Pardubice – 9 March 1982 Prague
Architect, graduated from the Czech Institute of Technology and the
Academy of Fine Arts in Prague. An editor of *Stavitel* magazine, worked
for Josef Gočár and later set up his own office. A member of Czechoslovak
CIAM Group. From 1945 until 1968 was a professor at the Institute of
Decorative Arts in Prague.

Matěj Blecha
16 July 1861 Štíťary – 18 December 1919 Prague
Builder and architect, owner of a Prague building firm. Studied at Prague
and Viennese technical schools and at Vienna Academy of Fine Arts.
Employed in his project office a number of important architects and
artists including Emil Králíček, Oldřich Tyl and a sculptor Čelda Klouček.
Erected and collaborated on several important Secessionist and Cubist
buildings.

Josef Chochol
13 December 1880 Písek – 6 July 1956 Prague
Architect, studied at the Czech Institute of Technology in Prague under
Professor Josef Schulz and at Vienna Academy of Fine Arts under Otto
Wagner. A member of Skupina výtvarných umělců, Mánes and Devětsil.
Chochol was one of the main Cubist architects and created many fine
examples in the Vyšehrad area of Prague. Soon after he came under the
influence of Purism and Functionalism, best reflected in unrealised
projects such as the remarkable proposal for Osvobozené divadlo (Liberated Theatre), 1927.

Jaroslav Fragner
25 December 1898 Prague – 3 January 1967 Prague
Architect, studied at the Czech Institute of Technology in Prague but did not finish the course. In 1922 he set up his own architectural practice in Prague. A Devětsil member, one of the first to turn to international Functionalism.

Jan Gillar
24 June 1904 Příbor – 7 May 1967 Prague
Architect, graduated from the Czech Institute of Technology in Prague. Worked for the building firm Záruba & Pfefferman, a member of Devětsil. In 1931 Gillar set up his own practice in Prague after winning the French Schools project.

Josef Gočár
13 March 1880 Semín u Pardubic – 10 September 1945 Jičín
Architect, urbanist and teacher, studied at the Industrial Arts School and afterwards at the Institute of Decorative Arts under Professor Jan Kotěra. After studies he joined Kotěra's studio. A member of Skupina výtvarných umělců and later Mánes. The main protagonist of Czech rational Modernism, Cubism and Functionalism.

Josef Havlíček
5 May 1899 Prague – 30 December 1961 Prague
Architect, studied at the Czech Institute of Technology and Academy of Fine Arts under Professor Josef Gočár. A member of Devětsil, Levá fronta and, from 1929, of CIAM. Exceptional Functionalist architect, collaborated with Honzík on several important projects between 1928 and 1936.

Vlastislav Hofman
6 February 1884 Jičín – 28 August 1964 Prague
Architect, painter, furniture designer, scenographic designer, studied at
the Czech Institute of Technology, a member of Artěl, Mánes and Skupina
výtvarných umělců. Hofman was awarded a gold medal at the Paris Decorative Arts Exhibition in 1925, a great prize at the Art and Technology
Exhibition in Paris in 1937 and at the Milan Trienale in 1940. An important exponent of Czech architectural Cubism. Most of his Prague projects
were unrealised.

Karel Honzík
24 September 1900 Le Croisic – 4 February 1966 Prague
Architect, furniture designer, graphic artist and writer. Honzík graduated
from the Czech Institute of Technology and became a member of Devětsil.
In 1928 he set up a practice with Josef Havlíček. Honzík was a supporter
of international Functionalism, and reinforced the view that artistic attitudes enhance the utilitarian character of architecture. Author of *Tvorba
životního stylu* (1946) and *Ze života avantgardy* (1963).

Karel Hubáček
23 February 1924 Prague
Architect and teacher, graduated from the Czech Institute of Technology
in Prague and worked for Stavoprojekt in Liberec from 1949. He established and managed Studio 2 SIAL within the Stavoprojekt in 1958 and
was awarded the Auguste Perret Prize by the UIA in Buenos Aires in 1969.
Hubáček is an exponent of Czech modern architecture of the high-tech
and futuristic styles. Other members of Studio 2 SIAL included Miroslav
Masák, Martin Rajniš, John Eisler, Emil Přikryl and Jiří Suchomel.

Pavel Janák
12 March 1882 Prague – 1 August 1956 Prague
Architect, furniture designer, urbanist and theoretician, studied at the
Czech Institute of Technology in Prague under Professor Josef Schulz and
at the Vienna Academy of Fine Arts under Otto Wagner. Janák worked
for Jan Kotěra between 1908 and 1909. A member of Mánes, Skupina
výtvarných umělců, an editor of art magazine *Výtvarná práce*, a professor
at the Institute of Decorative Arts from 1921 to 1942. The chief architect
of Prague Castle following Jože Plečnik in 1936. A founding architect of
Czech Cubism and Functionalism.

Jan Kaplický
18 April 1937 Prague
Architect, studied at the Institute of Decorative Arts and worked for the
State Design Office and on private projects. In 1968 he left Prague and
settled in Great Britain. After practising at Denys Lasdun, Piano & Rogers
and Foster Associates, in 1979 Kaplický set up an influential avant-garde
practice, Future Systems, with David Nixon. Kaplický has participated
in numerous international competitions. Recently, in partnership with
Amanda Levete, Kaplický has had the opportunity to realise some of his
designs.

Jan Kotěra
18 December 1871 Brno – 17 April 1923 Prague
Architect, painter and teacher, a founder of Czech modern architecture.
He graduated from the German Industrial Arts School in Plzeň and the
Vienna Academy of Fine Arts under Professor Otto Wagner. Received the
Rome Scholarship Prize in 1897, and was a member of Mánes. His archi-

tecture was influenced by trips abroad to the USA, Holland and Great Britain. A professor at the Institute of Decorative Arts and Academy of Fine Arts in Prague and a highly influential teacher of the next generation of Czech architects.

Emil Králíček
1877 Německý Brod – 1930 Prague
Architect, studied at Prague Industrial Arts School and privately with Antonín Balšánek in Prague and Josef Maria Olbrich in Darmstadt. He worked for several builders in Prague, mainly in the project office of Matěj Blecha. Králíček was one of the first architects to use Cubist forms.

Jaromír Krejcar
25 July 1895 Hundsheim – 5 October 1949 London
Architect, furniture designer, graphic artist, theoretician, teacher and editor. He studied at Prague Academy of Fine Arts under Professor Jan Kotěra. A Bauhaus representative in Czechoslovakia. Krejcar was married to Milena Jesenská, Franz Kafka's former friend. As an active Devětsil member he was a dedicated advocate of Purism and Functionalism. From 1948 Krejcar taught at the Architectural Association School in London.

Ludvík Kysela
25 April 1883 Kouřim – 10 February 1960 Prague
Architect and urbanist. He studied at the Czech Institute of Technology and created a number of the best commercial and retail buildings in Czech Functionalist style in Prague.

Evžen Linhart
20 March 1898 Kouřim – 29 December 1949 Prague
Architect, furniture designer and painter, studied at the Czech Institute of Technology in Prague, a member of Mánes and Devětsil. A talented architect and exponent of Purism and Functionalism. Linhart was strongly influenced by Le Corbusier's work.

Adolf Loos
10 February 1870 Brno – 22 August 1933 Vienna
Architect, furniture designer and theoretician, Loos studied at Dresden College of Technology. Between 1893 and 1896 he travelled in the USA and on his return he settled in Vienna. In 1908 Loos published his important essay *Ornament und Verbrechen* and later established his own School of Architecture. A greatly influential founder of three-dimensional space concept design and rational modern architecture. Villa Müller in Prague is one of his finest works.

Otakar Novotný
11 January 1880 Benešov – 4 April 1959 Prague
Architect and author, studied at the Institute of Decorative Arts under Professor Jan Kotěra and later worked in Kotěra's studio. A member of Mánes and a professor at the Institute of Decorative Arts. Initially Novotný was influenced by the Dutch architect, Hendrik P. Berlage, later becoming an important representative of Czech rational Modernism, Cubism and Functionalism. Novotný published *Jan Kotěra a jeho doba* in 1958.

Prague: a guide to twentieth-century architecture

Jože Plečnik
23 January 1872 Ljubljana – 6 January 1957 Ljubljana
Slovenian architect, furniture designer and urbanist, studied at Graz
Technical School and under Otto Wagner at the Vienna Academy of Fine
Arts with Kotěra, winning Rome Scholarship in 1898. Plečnik built in
Vienna and in 1911 was invited by Kotěra to Prague to teach at the Insti-
tute of Decorative Arts. From 1921 Plečnik taught at Ljubljana Univer-
sity. In 1920 Plečnik was commissioned by the Czechoslovak President
Tomáš G. Masaryk to work on the remodelling of Prague Castle. This
work continued until 1934. His other major project in Prague is the
Church of the Sacred Heart.

Osvald Polívka
24 May 1859 Enns – 30 April 1931 Prague
Architect, studied at the Czech Institute of Technology in Prague. Polívka
was an assistant to architect Josef Zítek who designed Prague National
Theatre. Polívka created a number of important Secessionist buildings in
Prague.

Eugene Rosenberg
24 February 1907 Topolčianky – 21 November 1990 London
Architect, studied engineering in Bratislava, Brno and Prague and architecture at Prague Academy of Fine Arts. Rosenberg worked for Le
Corbusier and for Havlíček and Honzík. Later he established a private
practice designing a number of important Functionalist buildings. In
1939 Rosenberg came to Britain where he met F.R.S. Yorke and a Finn,
Cyril Mardall (Sjöström). In 1944, they founded an architectural practice, Yorke Rosenberg and Mardall, in London.

Kamil Roškot
29 April 1882 Vlašim – 12 July 1945 Paris
Architect and painter, studied at the German University, Czech Institute of Technology and Academy of Fine Arts in Prague, a member of Mánes. In 1922 he opened his own practice in Prague. Roškot was awarded a gold medal for the Czechoslovak Pavilion, Milan in 1927. A classical Modernist and influential architect.

Otto Rothmayer
28 February 1892 Prague – 24 September 1966 Prague
Carpenter and architect. Studied at the Institute of Decorative Arts under Jože Plečnik. Later Rothmayer collaborated with Plečnik at Prague Castle, continuing his work (1921–56), and on the Sacred Heart Church.

Pavel Smetana
25 February 1900 Zákupy – 8 June 1986 Prague
Architect, furniture designer and theoretician. He graduated from the School of Industrial Arts and Prague Academy of Fine Arts studying under Professors Pavel Janák and Josef Gočár. A member of Devětsil. Smetana used unusual plastic and sculptural forms in his architectural work.

Oldřich Starý
15 March 1884 Prague – 3 November 1971 Prague
Architect and writer, and a professor at the School of Industrial Arts in Prague. An editor of magazines *Stavba* and *Architektura ČSR*.

Rudolf Stockar
28 May 1886 Doloplazy na Moravě – 19 December 1957 Prague

Architect, furniture and applied art designer, graduated from the Czech Institute of Technology in Prague. Director of Artěl. A Cubist, Purist and Functionalist architect.

Oldřich Tyl
12 April 1884 Ejpovice – 4 April 1939 Prague
Architect, studied at the Czech Institute of Technology in Prague and initially worked in Matěj Blecha's project office. Tyl established his own practice in 1913 and later founded the Tekta Cooperative of Architects and Builders. An author of several pioneering projects of Functionalist architecture.

František Zelenka
8 June 1904 Kutná Hora – 19 October 1943 Auschwitz
Architect, interior, stage and graphic designer, studied at the Czech Institute of Technology in Prague, a member of Devětsil. His main body of work was in the stage designs for theatre productions, including a fruitful cooperation with playwrights and actors Jiří Voskovec and Jan Werich at the avant-garde Osvobozené divadlo. His posters for Aero automobiles and v+w plays were particularly influential.

Ladislav Žák
25 June 1900 Prague – 26 May 1973 Prague
Architect and furniture designer, graduated from Prague Academy of Fine Arts. He founded his own office in Prague in 1930. Žák produced some of the finest examples of modern family villas in Prague.

Devětsil
A group of avant-garde artists which included architects, painters, photographers, writers and poets, Devětsil was established by the writer and painter Karel Teige in 1920 as a platform for Functionalistic Modernism. The work of the group influenced all Czech artistic and literary forms of expression. Devětsil broke up in 1931.

Mánes – Spolek výtvarných umělců (Mánes – Association of Fine Artists)
An association of artists founded in 1887 to evaluate and discuss the latest developments in European art, which published a magazine, *Volné směry*, and organised exhibitions. The group was named after Josef Mánes (1820–1871), a founder of Czech national painting style of the new era.

Skupina výtvarných umělců (Group of Fine Artists)
A group of painters, architects, sculptors and writers actively supporting the Cubist style between 1911 and 1914. They published their own magazine, *Umělecký měsíčník*.

Index

Prague: a guide to twentieth-century architecture

Academy of Fine Arts, Prague 294, 295, 298, 301
Academy of Fine Arts, Vienna 294, 297, 300
Adam Pharmacy 84
Adam Store 80
ADNS
  Office Centre Vinohrady **128**
Adriatica Palace 68, 72
Aero cars 110, 302
Agricultural Institute 130
Airport Lighthouse, Kbely **276**
Alda, Václav 80, 128
Aleš, Mikoláš 48
Alfa Arcade **92**
Apartment Building, Čechova **256**
Apartment Building, Kamenická **250**
Apartment Building, Letohradská **260**
Apartment Building, Neklanova **148**
Apartment Building, Schnirchova **246**
Apartment Buildings, Štěpánská **104**
ARA Department Store 66, **68**
Arcade, Štěpánská **104**
Arch, Spálená **112**
Architectural Association School of Architecture, London 298
Architektura ČSR (magazine) 301
Artěl **296**
Assicurazioni Generali & Moldavia Generali Building **58**
ASUM 192
'At the Black Madonna' Department Store **46**
'At the Black Rose' House **62**
'At the God's Eye' House **50**

'At the Golden Chair' House **40**
Atelier 8000 50
Aulický, Václav 11

Baba Villas **214–218**
Babuška, Milan 68
  National Technical Museum **262**
Bachner Department Store (Ostrava) 10
Bakery, U továren **290**
Balšánek, Antonín 298
  Obecní dům **48**
Bank of the Czechoslovak Legions **56**
Barrandov Film Studios 180, **192**
Barrandov Restaurant **196**
Baťa Building 84, 116
Baťa Department Store **86**
Baťa Project Office **86**
Baťa, Tomáš 86
Bauhaus 298
Bayer, Jan and Josef 154
Bechyně, Stanislav
  Lucerna Palace **106**
Behrens, Peter 10
Belada, Antonín 154
  Apartment Building, Neklanova **148**
Benš, Adolf 294
  Electricity Company Building **244**
  Old Prague Airport Terminal **236**
  Villa, Trojská **266**
Berlage, Hendrik Petrus 9, 42, 134, 299
Betlémská Chapel 7
Bílá hora (White Mountain) 7
Bílá Labuť Department Store **54**
Bílek, František 160
  Villa Bílek **202**

Blažek, Zdeněk 218
Blecha, Matěj 84, 206, 294, 302
    Diamant House **112**
    Moravian Bank **96**
Bočan, Josef 136
Bondy Department Store **62**
Bouda, Cyril 214
Breton, André 9
Breuer, Marcel 10
Brno Bank **100**
Broadway Arcade **58**
Broggio, Ottavio 112
Brokoff, Jan Michal 112
Brouk and Babka 54
Brožek, Vlastimil
    Music Store **72**
Brunner, Vratislav H. 24
Brychtová, Jaroslava 24
Bubeníček, Karel 236
Bulovka Hospital Dermatology Pavilion
    274

Caisse des Depots et Consignations 60
Čapek, Josef 96
Čapek, Karel 96
Cemetery, Ďáblice **272**
Černá Růže Arcade **62**
Černý, Antonín
    Assicurazioni Generali & Moldavia
        Generali Building **58**
Černý, František M.
    Church Tower, Na Slovanech **140**
Černý, Radko
    Hotel Praha **224**
Chareau, Pierre 110

Charles Bridge 7
Charles iv, King 7, 26
Charles University Extension **44**
Chicago Building 116
Chochol, Josef 148, 162, 220, 294
    Hodek Apartment Building **150**
    Hodek, Bayer and Belada House **154**
    Villa Kovařovič **146**
Church of Holy Trinity 112
Church of Our Lady of the Snow 72,
    84
Church of St Nicholas 20
Church of St Wenceslas **288**
Church of the Sacred Heart 10, **162**, 300,
    301
Church of the Virgin Mary and Saints
    Jeronym, Cyril and Metoděj 140
Church Tower, Na Slovanech **140**
Chytilová, Věra 268
CIAM **294**, 295
City Mayor's Hall, Municipal House 48
ČKD Building 66
Comenius, Jan Amos 8
Commercial Building, Rašínovo nábřeží
    138
Conk, Vladimír 236
Cooperative Housing, Elišky
    Krásnohorské **38**
Cubr, František
    Restaurant Praha Expo 58 **264**
Czech Broadcasting Company 128
Czech Institute of Technology 8, 294,
    295, 296, 297, 298, 299, 300, 301,
    302
Czech Lawn Tennis Club 242

Prague: a guide to twentieth-century architecture

Czech Museum of Fine Arts 46
Czechoslovak Decorative Arts Federation Building **116**
Czechoslovak Decorative Arts Federation 214
Czechoslovak Republic 9

D.A. Studio
    Speech Therapy Clinic **184**
Ďáblické hřbitovy 272
Danda, Josef 136
Department Store, Provaznická **64**
Devětsil 9, 98, 102, 114, 198, 234, 294, 295, 296, 298, 299, 301, 303
Děvín hill 188
Diamant House **112**
Doesburg, Theo van 9
Dresden College of Technology 299
Drobný, Zdeněk
    Malostranská Metro Station **32**
Dryák, Alois 94, 142
Dubček, Alexander 10
Duiker, Johannes 10
Dvořák, Karel 100
Dvořák, Petr 80, 128

Edison Transformer **98**
Ehrmann, Leopold
    Kafka's Tomstone **166**
Eisler, John 296
    Máj Department Store **118**
Electricity Company Building **244**
Emperor Franz-Josef Station 136
Engel, Antonín
    Water Filtration Works **170**

Falout, Josef 184
Fanta, Josef
    Hlahol House **122**
    Prague Main Railway Station **136**
Fencl, Vladimír 11
Ferdinand II, King 7
Filsák, Karel 236
Fišer, Jaroslav and Karel 216
Foehr, Adolf
    Department Store, Provaznická **64**
Fragner, Jaroslav 295
    Charles University Extension **44**
    Merkur Palace **52**
Franc, Stanislav 11
Frank O. Gehry & Associates
    Commercial Building, Rašínovo nábřeží **138**
Franz Kafka's Tombstone **166**
French Schools **212**, 295
Frenzl, Jan D. 62
Frič, Martin 180
Frýda, Vladimír
    Primary and Secondary Schools, Špitálská **280**
Fuchs, Josef 218
    Prague Trade Fair Palace **248**
Fürth, Viktor 258
Future Systems 297
    Memorial to the Victims of Communism **36**

Gehry, Frank 11
General Pensions Institute **158**
German Industrial Arts School 297
German occupation 10

Gillar, Jan 295
  Bílá Labuť Department Store **54**
  French Schools **212**
  'Glass Palace' (Provincial Bank
    Apartment Building) 208
Glücklich, Julius 214
Gočár, Josef 150, 294, 295, 216, 218,
  234, 295, 301
  Agricultural Institute **130**
  'At the Black Madonna' Department
    Store **46**
  Bank of the Czechoslovak Legions **56**
  Brno Bank **100**
  Hofmann & Stach Twin House **204**
  St Wenceslas Church **288**
Gottwald, President Klement 160
Grand Hotel Evropa **94**
Graz Technical School 300
Gregor, Čeněk
  Hlahol House **122**
Grégr, Vladimír 222
  Barrandov Restaurant **196**
  Villa, Barrandovská **194**
Gropius, Walter 9
Gutfreund, Otto 56, 74, 76, 240, 256
Gymnasium, Polská **132**

Habich Building **102**
Hanel, Lubomír 32
Hapsburgs 7, 8
Havel, President Václav 106, 124, 138
Havlíček, Josef 116, 258, 296, 300
  Apartment Building, Letohradská
    260
  General Pensions Institute **158**

Habich Building **102**
Molochov Apartment Buildings **258**
Villa Jíše **188**
Herbst, František 46
Heythum, Antonín 216
Hilbert, Kamil
  St Vitus Cathedral **24**
Hlahol House **122**
Hlava Pathology Institute **144**
Hlava, Jaroslav 144
Hlávkův most, *see* Josef Hlávka Bridge
Hlávka, Josef 240
Hlavní nádraží (Main Railway Station)
  136
Hodek Apartment Building 148, **150**
Hodek, Bayer and Belada House **154**
Hodek, František 154
Hofman, Vlastislav 84, 142, 150, 296
  Cemetery, Ďáblice **272**
Hofmann & Stach Twin House **204**
Hollar, Wenceslas 8
Hölzel, Zdeněk
  Myslbek Development **60**
Honzík, Karel 296, 300
  General Pensions Institute **158**
  Villa Jíše **188**
  Villa Langer **176**
Hotel Central 94
Hotel Don Giovanni 11
Hotel Hilton Atrium 11
Hotel Hoffmeister 11
Hotel International 10
Hotel Jalta 10
Hotel Juliš **90**
Hotel Meran **94**

Prague: a guide to twentieth-century architecture

Hotel Praha **224**
House of Artists (Rudolfinum) 8
Hradčany 8
Hrubý, Josef
  Restaurant Praha Expo 58 **264**
  Bílá Labuť Department Store **54**
Hubáček, Karel 286, 296
  Old Prague Airport Terminal **236**
  Water Pressure Equalisation Tower **190**
Hus, Jan 7
Hussite Congregation Church and
  Apartment Building **284**
Hypšman, Bohumil
  Bakery, U továren **290**
  Grand Hotel Evropa **94**
  Social Security and Health Ministries
  142

Industrial Arts School 295
Institute of Decorative Arts 18, 294, 295,
  297, 298, 299, 300, 301

Janák, Pavel 150, 166, 216, 218, 234,
  297, 301
  Baba Villas **214**
  Hotel Juliš **90**
  Hussite Congregation Church and
  Apartment Building **284**
  Josef Hlávka Bridge **240**
  Riunione Adriatica di Sicurtà Palace **74**
  Škoda Works Administrative Building
  76
Janů, Karel
  Winklerová Retail and Apartment
  Building **254**

Jarolím, Jan
  U Stýblů Building **92**
Jelení příkop (Deer Moat) 30
Jeřábek, František 10
Jesenská, Milena 298
Jirásek Square 138
Jirásková, Marta 260
Jiřičná, Eva
  Orangery **30**
Jiří z Poděbrad, King 26
Jirsák, Zbyněk
  Gymnasium **132**
Josef Hlávka Bridge **240**
Jungmann Square 82, 100
Jurkovič, Dušan 206

Kafka, Bohumil 48, 160
Kafka, Franz 166, 298
  Memorial Plaque **178**
  Tombstone **166**
Káleš, Josef
  Tennis Stadium **242**
Kalivoda, Ladislav
  Villa Traub **228**
Kamberský, Vladimír
  Church Tower, Na Slovanech
  140
Kaňka, František M. 44
Kaplický, Jan 36, 297
  Memorial to the Victims of
  Communism **36**
  Villa Dvořák **178**
Kaplický, Josef 288
Kapsa & Müller 230
Karlík, Josef 11

Karlovo náměstí Metro Station 32
Kavalier Glass Works 120
Kavalír, František 216
Keil, Petr 11
Kerel, Jan
  Myslbek Development **60**
Kerhart, František 216, 218
Kerhart, Vojtěch 216
Kincl, Petr
  Pragobanka Development **286**
Kittrich, Josef
  Bílá Labuť Department Store **54**
Klouček, Čelda 294
K-Mart 118
Kohn, Otto and Karel 258
Kolátor, Václav
  Swimming Pool, Barrandov **198**
Kordovský, Petr
  'At the God's Eye' House **50**
Koruna Palace **80**
Kotěra, Jan 18, 42, 150, 190, 256, 290,
  295, 297, 298, 299, 300
  Laichter House **134**
  Peterka Department Store **88**
  Urbánek House **78**
  Villa Kotěra **282**
  Villa Sucharda **206**
  Water Tower **174**
Koula, Jan 206, 216
  Svatopluk Čech Bridge **34**
Kousal, Radim
  Pragobanka Development **286**
Kozák, Bohumír
  Assicurazioni Generali & Moldavia
    Generali Building **58**

Králíček, Emil 96, 146, 206, 294, 298
  Diamant House **112**
  Lamp Post, Jungmannovo náměstí **84**
Královská zahrada (Royal Garden) 30
Krejcar, Jaromír 102, 298
  Olympic Building **114**
  Society of Self-Employed Clerical
    Workers **128**
  Villa Gibian **210**
Kříž, Josef
  Electricity Company Building **244**
Křinecký, Viktorin 50
Krupauer, Martin 50
Kuča, Otakar
  Malostranská Metro Station **32**
Kučerová-Záveská, Hana 214, 216
Kuchař, Gustav
  Swimming Pool Stadium **172**
Kulka, Heinrich 80
Kupka, Pavel 120
Kysela, František 24, 116
Kysela, Ludvík 298
  Baťa Department Store **86**
  Lindt Department Store **82**
  U Stýblů Building **92**

Laichter, Jan 134
Lamp Post, Jungmannovo náměstí **84**
Langer, František 176
Lášek, Jiří 236
Lauermann, Leo 258
Le Corbusier 9, 10, 110, 188, 248, 299,
  300
Léger, Fernand 56
Lehmann, Fritz 72

Prague: a guide to twentieth-century architecture

Lesser Quarter, *see* Malá Strana
Letenské sady (Letná Orchards)
    264
Letná Plain 8, 258
Letzl, Jan
    Grand Hotel Evropa **94**
Levá fronta 295
Levete, Amanda 36, 297
Lhota, Karel
    Villa Müller **230**
    Villa Winternitz **186**
Libenský, Stanislav 24
Libra, František A.
    Edison Transformer **98**
Lindt Department Store **82**, 84, 116
Linhart, Evžen 216, 299
    Secondary School of Dr Beneš **226**
    Villa Linhart **222**
Loos, Adolf 6, 9, 10, 80
    Villa Müller **230–232**
    Villa Winternitz **186**
Louda, Jiří 236
Lucerna Palace **106**
Lurçat, André 9

Mach, Josef 128
Machoň, Ladislav 216
magistrála 10, 136
Maison de Verre 110
Máj Department Store (K-Mart) **118**
Malá Strana 7, 8
Malostranská Metro Station **32**
Mánes 9, 124, 294, 295, 296, 297, 299,
    301, 303
Mánes Building **124**

Mánes, Josef 303
Mardall, Cyril 300
Marek, František
    Gymnasium **132**
Margolius, Rudolf 36
Masák, Miroslav 296
    Máj Department Store **118**
Masaryk Embankment 124
Masaryk, President Tomáš Garrigue 18,
    300
Masaryk's Terrace 30
Mašek, Karel 206
Mayer, Jaroslav 11
Memorial to the Victims of Communism
    36
Mencl, František
    Josef Hlávka Bridge **240**
Mendelsohn, Erich 10
Mentberger, Jan
    Music Store **72**
Merkur Palace **52**
Meyer, Hannes 9
Mies van der Rohe, Ludwig 9
Milunić, Vlado 138
Mocker, Josef
    St Vitus Cathedral **24**
Molochov Apartment Buildings **258**
Moravian Bank **96**
most Svatopluka Čecha **34**
Mottl, Karel 122
Mozarteum 78
Mucha, Alphonse 24, 48
Mühlstein, Arnošt 258
Müller, František 230
Munch, Edvard 9

Municipal House **48**
Music Store **72**
Můstek Metro Station 68
Myslbek Development **60**
Myslbek, Josef Václav 48, 80

Nahálka, Ivo 11
Národní technické museum, *see* National Technical Museum
National Gallery of Modern Art 248
National Monument **160**
National Museum 8
National Technical Museum **262**
National Theatre 8
Nationale Nederlanden 138
Navrátil, Arnošt
  Hotel Praha **224**
NCC International AB 118
Němec, Martin 80, 128
New Town, *see* Nové Město
Nová Scéna National Theatre **120**
Nováček, Jan 11
Novák, Karel 48, 88
Novák, Vratislav K. 34
Nové Město 7, 8
Novotná, Jana
  Tennis Stadium **242**
Novotný, Otakar 96, 146, 150, 299
  Apartment Building, Kamenická **250**
  Cooperative Housing, Elišky
    Krásnohorské **38**
  Mánes Building **124**
  Štenc House **42**
  Water Tower and Airport Lighthouse
    276

Obecní dům **48**
Obrovský, Jakub 160
Odehnal, Antonín 84
Office Building, Liliová **40**
Office Centre Vinohrady **128**
Ohmann, Bedřich 94
Oko Cinema 252
Olbrich, Josef Maria 298
Old Prague Airport Terminal **236**
  Aircraft Maintenance Hanger 236
  Main Airport Terminal 236
Old Town Square, *see* Staroměstské náměstí
Old Town, *see* Staré Město
Olympic Building 102, **114**
Orangery **30**
'Ornament und Verbrechen' (Loos essay) 299
Osvobozené divadlo (Liberated Theatre) 110, 294, 302
Oud, J.J.P. 9, 10
Ozenfant, Amédée 9

Pacassi, Nicolo F.L. 28
Palace of Culture 11
Palacký Hall, Municipal House 48
Palacký Square 272
Palacký, František 142
Palacký Hall 48
Palička, Jiří 216
Papež, Gustav 206
Parent, Claude 11
  Myslbek Development **60**
Parler, Peter 24
Parliament Building 11

Prague: a guide to twentieth-century architecture

Paroubek, Jaroslav
Hotel Praha **224**
Patrman, Zdeněk
Water Pressure Equalisation Tower
190
Paul, Bruno 6
Villa Traub **228**
Pavlík, Karel 84
Pekárek, Josef 88, 122
Pelcl, Lubomír 32
Perret, Auguste 106
Pešan, Damian 162
Pešánek, Zdeněk 98
Peterka Department Store **88**
Pfeiffer, Antonín
Koruna Palace **80**
Plečnik, Jože 6, 10, 28, 30, 297, 300, 301
Church of the Sacred Heart **162**
Prague Castle **18–22**
Podzemný, Richard F.
Provincial Bank Apartment Building
208
Swimming Pool Stadium **172**
Pokorný, Karel 160
Pokorný, Zdeněk
Restaurant Praha Expo 58 **264**
Polívka, Jaroslav 116
Habich Building **102**
Polívka, Karel
Music Store **72**
Polívka, Osvald 300
Obecní dům **48**
U Nováků Palace **108**
Popp, Antonín 34
Porte Molitor apartments 110

Prager, Karel 11
Nová Scéna National Theatre **120**
Pragobanka Development **286**
Prague Academy of Fine Arts 298, 300,
301, 302
Prague Castle 6, 7, 10, **18–22**, 297, 300,
301
basin 20
Bastion Garden 18
Bellevue pavilion 20
Belvedere pavilion 20
First Courtyard 18
fountain 20
monolith 20
Moravian Bastion 20
Paradise Garden 20
Plečnik Hall 18
Ramparts Garden 20
Second Courtyard 18
Theresian Wing 28
Third Courtyard 18
Vilém Slavata z Chlumu monument 20
Prague Industrial Arts School 298
Prague Institute for Construction 120
Prague Main Railway Station **136**
Prague Trade Fair Palace **248**
Prague University 7
Praha Insurance Company 108
Prašný most (Powder Bridge) 30
Preisler, Jan 48, 108
President Wilson Station 136
Přikryl, Emil 296
Villa Chytilová **268**
Primary and Secondary Schools, Špitalská
280

Provincial Bank Apartment Building **208**

public transport 14

Rajniš, Martin 296
  Máj Department Store **118**
  Speech Therapy Clinic **184**
Rašín Embankment 124
Řehák, František
  ARA Department Store **68**
Restaurant Praha Expo 58 **264**
Retail and Apartment Building,
  Jungmannovo náměstí **70**
Retail and Apartment Building, Palackého
  110
Retail, Cinema and Apartment Buildings,
  Františka Křižíka **252**
Rieger Hall, Municipal House 48
Riegerovy sady 132, 136
Riunione Adriatica di Sicurta Palace **74**
Rodin, Auguste 9
Rosůlek, Jan
  Bulovka Hospital Dermatology
  Pavilion **274**
Rosenberg, Eugene 254, 300
  Apartment Building, Schnirchova
  246
  Apartment Buildings **104**
Roškot, Kamil 72, 301
  Apartment Building, Čechova **256**
  Old Prague Airport Terminal **236**
  Tombs of Czech Kings 26
Rosůlek, Jan 222
Rothmayer, Otto 164, 301
  Theresian Wing, Prague Castle **28**

Rotlev House, Charles University 44
Rudolf II, King 26

Sacred Heart Church, *see* Church of the
  Sacred Heart
Šafer, Jaroslav
  Office Building, Liliová **40**
St Jacob Church 50
St Salvator Church 42
St Vitus Cathedral 7, **24**, 232
  Tombs of Czech Kings **26**
St Wenceslas Church **288**
Šaloun, Ladislav 48, 136
Schlaffer, František
  Hlahol House **122**
School of Industrial Arts 301
Schulz, Josef 294, 297
Secondary School of Dr Beneš **226**
Sedláčková, Anna 192
Semper, Gottfried 18
SIAL 248, 296
  Máj Department Store **118**
  Pragobanka Development **286**
  Water Pressure Equalisation Tower **190**
Šítkovský water mill 124
Škoda Works Administrative Building **76**
Škoda cars 262
Skupina výtvarných umělců 150, 294,
  295, 296, 297, 303
Sláma, Bohumil 128
Slánský Trial 36
Slovanský Island 124
Smetana Concert Hall, Municipal House
  48
Smetana, Bedřich 122

Smetana, Pavel 301
  Villa, U Ladronky **234**
Social Security and Health Ministries **142**
'Socialism with a Human Face' 10
Society of Self-Employed Clerical
  Workers 128
Šolc, Josef
  Retail, Cinema and Apartment
  Buildings, Františka Křižíka **252**
Soukup, Jiří
  Svatopluk Čech Bridge **34**
Soviet occupation 10
Špála Gallery 110
Špalek, Alois
  Hlava Pathology Institute **144**
Španiel, Otakar 24
Speech Therapy Clinic 11, **184**
Špillar, Karel 48
Šrámek, Jan 136, 236
  ČKD Building **66**
Šrámková, Alena 136
  ČKD Building **66**
Střítecký, Jiří 50
Stam, Mart 6, 9, 10, 214, 216
Staré Město 7, 8
Starý, Oldřich 56, 216, 218, 301
  Czechoslovak Decorative Arts
  Federation Building **116**
State Design Office 297
State Institute for Reconstruction 120
Stavba (magazine) 301
Stavitel (magazine) 294
Stavovské Theatre 46
Stempel, Jan 80, 128
Štenc House **42**

Štenc, Jan 42
Štěpánská Arcade 246
Stirling, James 22
Stockar, Rudolf 72, 100, 301
  Retail and Apartment Building,
  Jungmannovo náměstí **70**
Stockar-Bernkop, Jaroslav
  Retail, Cinema and Apartment
  Buildings, Františka Křižíka **252**
Streets and Squares
  Anglická 128
  Barrandovská 194, 196, 198
  Božkova 212
  Bubenská 240, 244
  Bulovka 274
  Čechova 256
  Charlese de Gaulla 210
  Charvátova 116
  Chopinova 134
  Ďáblická 272
  Dukelských hrdinů 248
  Dykova 284
  Elišky Krásnohorské 38
  Evropská 226
  Francouzská 128
  Františka Křižíka 252
  Hanusova 174
  Hradešínská 134, 282
  Hybernská 94
  Jarní 216
  Jelení příkop 30
  Jeruzalemská 98
  Jindřišská 100
  Jungmannovo náměstí 70, 72, 74, 76,
    78, 134

Streets and Squares (continued)
K letišti 236
Kamenická 250
Klárov 32
Kostelní 262
Kříženeckého náměstí 192
Laubkova 162
Lazarská 112
Letohradská 260
Libušina 146
Liliová 40
Maiselova 178
Malá Štupartská 50
Masarykovo nábřeží 122, 124
Mickiewiczova 202
Mikulandská 50
Milady Horákové 228, 254, 258
Mladoboleslavská 276
Na Babě 216
Na Cihlářce 186
Na Dobešce 178
Na lysinách 180
Na Míčance 220
Na ostrohu 216
Na poříčí 56, 54
Na příkopě 58, 60
Na viničních horách 222
Na vysočanských vinicích 278
Na Zátorce 206
Nad cementárnou 176
Nad hradním vodojemem 232
Nad Paťankou 218
Nad vodovodem 166
Náměstí Jiřího z Poděbrad 164
Náměstí Republiky 48

Náměstí Svatopluka Čecha 288
Náměstí Svobody 208
Náměstí W. Churchilla 158
Národní 108, 116, 118, 120
Neherovská 220
Neklanova 148, 152
Ostrov Štvanice 242
Ovocný trh 44, 46
Palackého 110, 142
Panská 62
Pařížská 34
Perlová 68
Pod Havránkou 268
Pod hradbami 228
Podolská 170, 172
Polská 132
Pražská vodárny 190
Pražský hrad 22, 24, 26, 28, 30
Provaznická 64
Průhledová 218
Rašínovo nábřeží 138, 154
Revoluční 52
Římská 128
Salvátorská 42
Schnirchova 246
Skalní 194
Slavíčkova 206
Slezská 130
Spálená 112, 114, 118
Špitalská 280
Staroměstské náměstí 7, 178
Starostrašnická 286
Štěpánská 96, 102, 104, 106
Studničkova 144
Suchardova 206

Prague: a guide to twentieth-century architecture

Prague: a guide to twentieth-century architecture

Streets and Squares (continued)
  Sušická 224
  Trojská 266
  28. října 70
  Tychonova 204
  U Dívčích hradů 188
  U Ladronky 234
  U Mrázovky 184
  U továren 290
  Václavské náměstí 80, 82, 86, 88, 90,
    92, 94, 96
  Ve Smečkách 246
  Vinohradská 286
  Vítkov 160
  Vodičkova 106, 108
  Vyšehradská 140
  Wilsonova 136
Štursa, Jan 56, 74, 78, 240
Štvanice Island 240, 242
Styles
  Art Nouveau 8
  Baroque 6
  Classicism 170
  Cubism 9, 38, 46, 72, 74, 78, 84,
    112, 130, 146, 148, 150, 152, 154,
    160, 162, 166, 204, 240, 256, 272,
    294, 295, 296, 297, 298, 299, 302,
    303
  Deconstructivism 50, 286
  Functionalism 68, 86, 104, 116, 124,
    128, 132, 158, 210, 222, 234, 266,
    294, 295, 296, 297, 298, 299, 300,
    302, 303
  Gothic 7, 72
  high-tech 40, 296

Modernism 9, 134, 146, 150, 256, 282,
  290, 295, 299, 301, 303
Neo-classicism 146
Post-modernism 11, 286
Purism 256, 298, 299, 302
Romanesque 7
Rondo-Cubism 38, 56, 70, 76, 100,
  250
Secession 6, 8, 48, 80, 84, 88, 94, 108,
  122, 134, 136, 150, 202, 206, 294,
  300
Socialist Realism 10
Sucharda, Stanislav 136, 142, 206
Sucharda, Vojtěch 80
Suchomel, Jiří 286, 296
Sutnar, Ladislav 214
Švabinský, Max 48, 160
Svatopluk Čech Bridge **34**, 36
Svaz československého díla
  (Czechoslovak Decorative Arts
  Federation) 214
Švec, Otakar 34
Swimming Pool Stadium **172**
Swimming Pool, Barrandov **198**

Talacko, Lubomír 32
Tatra 194, 262
taxis 14
Teige, Karel 198, 303
Tekta Cooperative of Architects and
  Builders 302
Tennis Stadium 11, **242**
Tenzer, Antonín 10
Theresian Wing, Prague Castle 28
Tombs of Czech Kings **26**

Topič House 108
Traub, Edmund 228
Tyl, Oldřich 294, 302
    Bondy Department Store and Černá
        Růže Arcade 62
    Prague Trade Fair Palace 248

U božího oka 50
U Hřebeckých 104
U Nováků Palace 108
U Špinků House 80
U Stýblů Building 92
Umělecký měsíčník (magazine) 303
Union Bank 60, 66
Unwin, Raymond 9
Urban, Max 180
    Barrandov Film Studios 192
    Barrandov Restaurant 196
Urbánek House 78, 134
Urbánek, Mojmír 78
Ustohal, Vladimír 11

Václav IV, King 26, 44
Vaněk, Antonín 11
Vejrych, Václav
    Gymnasium 132
Velde, Henry van de 9
Vilímek Publishers 110
Villa Balling 216
Villa, Barrandovská 194
Villa Barrová 220
Villa Bautz 216
Villa Bělehrádek 218
Villa Bílek 202
Villa Bouda 216

Villa Čeněk 216
Villa Chytilová 11, 268
Villa Dovolil 216
Villa Dvořák 178
Villa Frič 180
Villa Gibian 210
Villa Glücklich 216
Villa Hain 278
Villa Herain 216
Villa Heřman 216
Villa Janák 218
Villa Jiroušková 216
Villa Jíše 188
Villa Joska 216
Villa Košťál 216
Villa Kotěra 134, 282
Villa Kovařovič 146
Villa Kraus 206
Villa Kytlica 218
Villa Langer 176
Villa Letošník 216
Villa Lindová 216
Villa Linhart 222
Villa Lisý 216
Villa Lom 216
Villa Lužná 218
Villa Maule 218
Villa Moravcová 216
Villa Müller 10, 186, 230–232, 299
Villa Munk 218
Villa Palička 10, 216
Villa Peřina 216
Villa Poláček 216
Villa Procházka 202
Villa Řezáč 216

Villa Říha **184**
Villa Sequens 146
Villa Spíšek 216
Villa Sucharda **206**
Villa Suková 216
Villa Sutnar 218
Villa Traub **228**
Villa Tugendhat (Brno) 10
Villa Uhlíř 216
Villa Vaváček 216
Villa Verunáč 220
Villa Winternitz 10, **186**
Villa Zadák 216
Villa Zaorálek 216
Villa, Trojská **266**
Villa, U Ladronky **234**
Vltava river 6, 7, 196, 242, 264
Volné směry (magazine) 303
Voskovec, Jiří 108, 302
Vosmík, Čeněk 136, 288
Votava, František 258
Vršovice 288
Výtvarná práce (magazine) 297

Wagner, Otto 18, 56, 294, 297, 300
Waigant, Bohumil 134
Waldstein Equestrian School 32
Water Filtration Works **170**
Water Pressure Equalisation Tower **190**
Water Tower **174**
Water Tower, Mladoboleslavská **276**
Wenceslas Square 10, 80, 84, 92, 96, 106
Werich, Jan 108, 302
Winklerová Retail and Apartment Building **254**
Wright, Frank Lloyd 9, 42, 134
Wycliffe, John 7

Yerbury, Frank 9
Yorke Rosenberg and Mardall 300
Yorke, F.R.S. 9, 300

Žák, Ladislav 214, 216, 302
  Villa Frič **180**
  Villa Barrová **220**
  Villa Hain **278**
Záruba & Pfefferman 295
Zasche, Josef 66
  Riunione Adriatica di Sicurta Palace **74**
Zázvorka, Jan
  National Monument **160**
Zelenka, František 216, 302
  Czechoslovak Decorative Arts Federation Building **116**
  Retail and Apartment Building, Palackého **110**
Zemská banka (Provincial Bank) 208
Zhořelecký, Jan 26
Zítek, Josef 120, 300
Žižka, Jan 160
Žižka Monument 272
Žižkov radio jamming and TV tower 11